SOMEBODY MOVED

WRITTEN BY
COMBAT VIETNAM VETERAN
WILLIAM C. DRAPER

Elbert & Charla
We share such a wonderfull
Blessing I feel so blessed to
have Cindi & Cassidy in
our lives.
            God Bless You
               Bill

TATE PUBLISHING, LLC

Published in the United States of America
by Tate Publishing, LLC
127 East Trade Center Terrace
Mustang, OK 73064
(888) 361–9473

This book is designed to provide accurate and authoritative information with regard to the subject matter covered. This information is given with the understanding that neither the author nor Tate
Publishing, LLC is engaged in rendering legal, professional advice.
Since the details of your situation are fact dependent, you should
additionally seek the services of a competent professional.

ISBN: 1–9331487–2-1

DEDICATION

This book is dedicated to my cousin,
LCPL Robert Dale Draper,
who lost his life 2 August 1967 in Vietnam.

ACKNOWLEDGEMENTS

A special thank you . . .

. . . to my wife and all of her family for standing by me for over 30 years.

. . . to my sons and daughter-in-law for their love and help.

. . . to my mom and grandmother for their prayers, encouragement, and support throughout the years.

. . . to my brothers (Combat Veterans' Group)who meet with me each week and who have helped so much in the healing process.

. . . to my sister, C. Draper Wafford, for her many hours of research, transcribing, typing, and preliminary editing of this book.

. . . to my aunt, Jo Ann Coyer Plunk, for her conceptual cover idea for the novel.

TABLE OF CONTENTS

FOREWORD ONE

An intensely powerful story that needs to be told. Offers incredible insight and understanding for the families of Vietnam Veterans, and promotes healing for those who were there. Even if one's life has not been directly touched by Vietnam, this soldier's firsthand account is gripping, and he offers the true source of peace, strength, and redemption for all of us who fight life's daily battles.

Brian Cannon, Associate Pastor
Grace Vineyard Fellowship
Oklahoma City, OK

FOREWORD TWO

We, as sons of this Vietnam Veteran, knew very little of our dad's experiences in the war. He rarely spoke about his hidden feelings. After reading this novel, we understand so much better what our dad suffered through in Vietnam and how so many others have suffered and are continuing to suffer today.

How wonderful it is to have an account of our father's experiences written down and to know he is reaching out to help others. As we read the pages of this book, we could picture our dad as a young man and the physical and emotional battles he faced. It truly broke our hearts to read about the way the Vietnam Veterans were treated even after serving their time in Vietnam.

It was once written that Vietnam Veterans are the greatest men on the planet. We certainly believe that of our father and are so thankful and grateful for the combat veterans who served our Country and taught us what the word Patriot really means.

The proud sons of this Veteran,
Bill Draper
Jason Draper

FOREWORD THREE

This man I have known for only a few years has masterfully painted a vivid picture of the Vietnam War and the sovereignty of God. His own words prove that even the foolishness of men cannot change the will of our Lord. This book brings to life the reality of the Vietnam War and the hopelessness our soldiers felt and carried in their hearts as they followed the orders of their superiors.

Even so, we see that God's divine protection was evident, and He made His presence known even in the war-torn jungles of Vietnam. After reading this book, I see the disorganization of government involved in this war. That causes me to know and realize that any soldier who made it out of that war alive was a miracle. The facts and the personal experiences that are expressed in this account help me to understand our Vietnam Veterans and know better how to help and minister to them.

As I read this, the Spirit of God revealed many Truths concerning our own personal walk and how we must wage a good war for the Kingdom of God. I know that any individual who reads this book with an open heart will receive a new revelation of God's sovereignty and divine protection over his elect.

Reverend Doug Wilkins
May 11, 1965–September 26, 2003*
Dead to Sin; Alive in Christ
Romans 6:11

***Rev. Doug Wilkins died in an accident just a few days after my completion of this book. He will be greatly missed by so many of us whose lives he touched.**

Bear's Scripture that rode with us in our tank:
"Greater love has no one than this,
that he lay down his life for his friends."
1 John 15:13

. . . or his Country (added by Harlem's grandmother).

*The 11th Armored Cavalry lost 742 men in Vietnam.

One hundred thousand men and women have committed suicide since the war was over.

There are over 1,000 Vietnam Veterans a year who are still committing suicide.

Over 100,000 are homeless . . .

*General George Patton, Jr., died 27 June 2004.

INTRODUCTION

"O Sovereign God, my strong deliverer, who shields my head in the day of battle." Psalms 140:7

God's hand led mine so I could express the traumatic experiences of a Combat Veteran—the need to help families understand what has happened and what is continuing to happen to their Veterans. So many wives, mothers, siblings, and children of Vietnam Veterans are trying to help, but they don't know how. The first step begins with an understanding of the war and what we, as Veterans, carry with us each day. This is an attempt to give the reader an insight into some of the things we endured, from a first-hand account of those experiences.*

Combat Veterans of any war go through life differently than most people. We are changed forever with deep emotional wounds and scars. We feel a need to cover up our true feelings. We served our Country proudly, never realizing the guilt we would always carry. There was never any closure to the Vietnam War. We were not allowed to win, and the anger and unrest of the Country turned toward the troops. Vietnam was a living hell. When we returned home the torment did not end. The rejection and disapproval from our own Country was an added burden that we were not prepared to carry.

Most of us have never had the opportunity to see the Wall which has so many of our comrades' names on it. Someday, maybe . . .

Over 54,000 names of men and women are on the Wall. They gave all for their country. Over 100,000 are homeless and thousands have committed suicide.[1] The Veterans whom I know do not want pity, just understanding. Your outstretched hand may be all they need to pull them up.

A group of us recently received letters on Veteran's Day from some seventh and eighth grade students in my sister's classes. They thanked us for serving and for the sacrifices that we had made. It was such a moving experience for all of us. It was

19

the first time most of the men had ever been thanked from someone outside of their families. Four of us wanted to thank them
personally. Most of the group knew they couldn't speak, but the
students were very respectful and wanted us to talk to them. It
was very difficult for us as Combat Veterans of Vietnam. Most
were wounded, receiving several Purple Hearts. All are 100 percent disabled. We couldn't speak to junior high students. We're
all men in our 50s; most of us grandfathers. Some of us broke
down. We were so touched by what they had done. They were
taught respect for the Veteran and what we had been through.
This has been really important to us in the healing process.

I have received letters from women in their 50's—asking
for forgiveness for the way they treated us—for their protest-
ing and disrespect. Jesus made the ultimate sacrifice so that we
might all be forgiven.

I've had Combat Veterans call me who were crying and
asking for help—men who have made good careers for themselves, but their toughness has finally broken. They are pleading
for help. Our Government has programs in place to help, but it
takes time. Someone has to help them.

Below is a list of places to seek help from the Government.
If God lays it on your heart to help a veteran, take the light of
God with you. Jesus is the only true answer.

Pray for our troops serving our Country today. Your
prayer may be the one that brings them home. There is no doubt
that intercessory prayer from others sent a covering of angels to
protect and lead me through the fire of war.

DAV - Disabled American Veterans (859) 441–7300
VFW - Veterans of Foreign Wars (800) vfw-1899
PVA - Paralyzed Veterans of America (800) 824–8200
American Legion (202) 861–2700
All provide assistance at no charge to help the Veteran.

*Names have been changed to protect my comrades-in-
arms.

DEFINITION OF TERMS

AIT: Advanced Individual Training

AO: Area of Operations

APC: Armored Personnel Carrier

ARVN: Army of the Republic of Vietnam

Azimuth: Arc of the horizon measured clockwise from such a point to a vertical circle passing from the zenith through the center of a star

Basic Training: The first military training every soldier receives

Berm: Ledge or wall used to screen troops from enemy fire

Chinook: CH-47 transport helicopter

Claymore: A directional mine that can fill a fan-shaped area with shrapnel

CO: Commanding Officer

Comrades: Friends; close companions

Door Gunner: An infantryman who mans an M60 machine gun on a helicopter

Duffel bag: A large, waterproof canvas bag for carrying clothing

FO: Forward Observer–Spotter for artillery; one of the first men in the battle who can see the enemy and locate the enemy using coordinates to call in artillery

Frag: Hand grenade

FSB: Fire Support Base

Hooch: Makeshift sleeping quarters in Vietnam

Howitzer: A short cannon with a low muzzle velocity

HQ: Headquarters

KIA: Killed In Action

Kill Zone: Area in front of an ambush where the maximum firepower is directed

LRRP: Long Range Reconnaissance Patrol

LZ: Landing Zone

M16: Standard U.S. 5.56mm automatic rifle

M60: Standard U.S. 7.62mm machine gun

Medevac: A helicopter carrying EMT (emergency medical treatment) gear and medics, used for evacuation out of a combat zone—armed only with door gunners

Montagnard: The hill people of Vietnam

Mortar Rounds: A short-barreled cannon with a low muzzle velocity that hurls shells in a high trajectory

NCO: Noncommissioned officer

OCS: Officers' Candidate School

Perimeter: Boundary strip where defenses are set up

Reconnaissance: An exploratory survey to check out enemy positions; a preliminary survey of the area

RPG: Rocket Propelled Grenade

S2: Intelligence Officer

S3: Operations Officer

TC: Tank Commander

Tet: A three-day Asian festival in winter, celebrating the arrival of the New Year in accordance with the lunar calendar. The Tet offensive began in January of 1968 in Vietnam when the North Vietnamese broke the truce with the Americans and attacked several key cities and base camps.

TOP: First Sergeant

Trip Flare: Illuminating pyrotechnics designed to indicate enemy's location—triggered by a trip wire.

VC: Vietcong–Communist Soldier

WIA: Wounded In Action

WP: White phosphorus

XO: Executive Officer

CHAPTER 1

DRAFTED

"Everyone must submit himself to the governing authorities, for there is no authority except that which God has established . . . Therefore, it is necessary to submit to the authorities, not only because of possible punishment but also because of conscience." Romans 13: 1, 5

1967

Thirty-five years ago seems like forever . . . and yet it seems like only yesterday. I joined the U.S. Army after receiving a draft notice in July of 1967. I sought the advice of several WW II and Korean Veterans, one being my father, a Navy Veteran of both wars. I found advice very hard to come by; people who knew what war was didn't want to give advice because of the guilt they might bear if their advice resulted in death. I understand now, but then I just wanted someone to tell me what to do (go with the draft, join the Air Force, whatever).

My plans had been to go to junior college for two years and then join the Air Force, so I went to the Air Force recruiter. "It's July 6, and your reporting date to the draft is July 13." He laughed and continued, "Son, we have a six-month waiting list." I found the same treatment at the Navy and Coast Guard. I would have been able to join the Marines, so my decision came down to joining the Army. I made a three-year deal so I would get proper training, including specialty training that would better prepare me for war if I had to go.

I still left on July 13 for Fort Polk, Louisiana. I had heard lots of stories about the service and knew enough to do what I was told. I had lived a sheltered life and had no idea about the world. It did not take long to start learning. I was sick, lost, and devastated by what was happening to me. How could I have been dragging Main Street, acting like a teenager, enjoying my life, and now be standing on a yellow line in Louisiana being called all kinds of names that I would have fought over a week earlier? I stood there scared to death and said, "Yes, Drill Sergeant," while receiving my army-issued clothes.

A year earlier in my college speech class we were debating Vietnam. Even then, I didn't really take it seriously or pay much attention. I was suddenly realizing the seriousness of my situation. Basic was basic for everyone, whomever served our country, and there are endless stories about it. Naturally, I also have many stories, but the one that remains with me and stands out most of all is the day I waited in a long line to use the phone to call my parents.

I had only a few minutes to talk and could not get any answer, so I called my grandmother. When she answered, she told me where my parents were and that they had gone to Arizona. My first cousin, who had joined the Marines right after high school, was killed by machine gun fire near Danang, Vietnam. His 16-man platoon had all been slaughtered. He had joined under what they called the "buddy system." Nine young men all joined the marines together out of high school. All went to Vietnam. Six came back in body bags. Things were really beginning to sink in and I was scared not knowing what was in store for me.

The other thing I had realized was that I wasn't the only one affected. I had seen the strain, worry, stress, and pain it placed on my family. My cousin's family was completely torn apart and destroyed by his death. My life had changed more than I could have ever imagined.

Basic lasted for another four weeks, and I had met and lived with guys from everywhere and from every background imaginable. Some were married and had children. They came from all walks of life. I felt sorry for them. None of us knew what we were facing, except Vietnam, and what was happening there was a hot topic.

After graduating from basic training, my orders sent me to Ft. Sill, Oklahoma, for the Survey Training. (I had signed an extra year to get it.) I felt somewhat better. I would be able to see my future wife and my family some. I met guys from Texas and Oklahoma, but the ones from New Jersey, New York, Maryland, and other places up North were quite a treat to listen to as I learned a little about them and where they lived. I still have never seen those places, but I remember their stories well.

We went through the steps of eight weeks of Survey Training. Many had not been able to cut all of the math we had in the surveying of artillery targets and map reading. They became cooks remaining in Ft. Sill cooking for trainees. I wrote home once saying that might not have been a bad idea, but I had been in long enough to know that cooking was hard, and the guys worked long hours. I had a few times at KP so that kept me from yearning to cook. I decided to just take my chances since I had graduated AIT and was a surveyor.

As the training ended, we knew we would be getting our orders in a few days. About every other group was going to either Germany or Vietnam, but no groups had been split up. We knew we would all be going to one place or the other. On graduation day, we got our orders, and I still recall the way I felt when I heard where my group would be going—Vietnam—a word, a destination, a war, a reality—a devastation that has lived with me ever since that day in November of 1967.

We all wondered what had happened. An extra year in the Army and after only a few months of training, we were on our way to Vietnam. They gave us 30 days of leave, right before Christmas. What a sick feeling. What had happened to me? What went wrong? My life wasn't supposed to be like this. Friends at home were still in school, still working, and still unsure of what was ahead of them. I advised them to do what they could to get in the National Guard, Reserves, or the Air Force. Some took my advice, and some just got lucky. Their destinies were to be much different from mine. I started looking for reasons. Why me? I had been in college; I should never have been drafted. I should have asked questions and not submitted so easily.

I thought about the summers spent with my cousin—playing, riding horses, swimming, and just having fun. He had given his ALL for our Country in a foreign place across the ocean. I didn't understand why, except that our government asked him to go . . . and he went. I had another cousin that was older than we were. He was 26 but still eligible for the draft. He decided to just go with the two years the Army gave him. He was now in Ft. Polk, Louisiana, Tiger Land Infantry Training. It sure looked like an unfair world to me. It seemed like all my family had to serve when so many others did not. I was really scared, but I wasn't going to admit it to anyone. I was still ignorant about everything and had no opinions about the world situation. I didn't really watch much television; I just knew it was real. I wasn't really bitter about the guys seeking a way out, but I thought running to Canada was unforgivable. I still have trouble with that.

When I saw people in town, they'd ask, "Where are they sending you?"

I would proudly answer, "Vietnam. I'm going to do my part."

Most said, "Good luck." The older men had a look in their eyes that I would never forget. A real sadness came over them, and I could see through their eyes what war was. They didn't try to tell me anything. They just showed their love, and I could tell they knew where I was going. There really wasn't any way to tell someone about war, and if you've really experienced it, you didn't want to talk about it.

All my family and my future wife tried to have a good Christmas. It was also a memory I will never forget. All the pictures, the tears—it was a sad time. The ride to the airport was difficult for all of us. My dad, mom, sister, and fiancée took me. I flew out of Oklahoma City expecting a layover in California. I would leave the next day for Vietnam.

Our first stop was somewhere near Oakland. Talk about a culture shock! I was an "Okie" seeing California for the first time. I saw more black guys than I had ever seen in my life; some of them were wearing T-shirts that read "Black Power" and had a clenched fist on them. I asked one guy on the bus what that meant, and he said, "I ain't sure, but we better stay on the bus." It looked more dangerous on the streets of Oakland than any place I had ever been.

After arriving at an Air Force Base, we spent one night before catching a commercial plane to Vietnam. I looked around and found a few guys that I had been with in Fort Sill.

It was December 22, 1967. We left Oakland that morning for a long flight over the ocean. It was the first time I had ever seen the ocean, any ocean. I've still never put my foot in it. We landed for refueling somewhere in Japan late at night. We left from there for Vietnam. It was a short trip. We could see mortar rounds exploding and artillery being fired, and we could hear some machine gun fire as we landed.

CHAPTER 2

REALITY OF VIETNAM

I say to God my Rock, "Why have you forgotten me? Why must I go about mourning, oppressed by the enemy?" My bones suffer mortal agony as my foe taunts me, saying to me all day long, "Where is your God?" Psalms 42:9–10

DECEMBER 23, 1967

It had been cold when we left the world. I went to the plane door and overheard the stewardesses talking. "We need to get these guys off. We have body bags again."

Another said, "I hate this stuff."

As I stood on the threshold at the door, it felt like I had stuck my head into an oven. I couldn't breathe. It was two or three o'clock in the morning and still so hot it seemed unbearable. The smell was unbelievable. I'd never smelled dead people. The air was full of the stench; death, sewer, gunpowder, and diesel fuel. It felt like the air itself was going to kill us.

They had told us to hurry and find our duffel bags and put them under a pavilion, which they had set up by the airstrip. I looked for mine in a large pile, finally finding it. Some twenty yards away, I saw what seemed to be an endless pile of body bags—all black and shiny. They had begun to

29

load them onto the plane that we had just left. Then I heard a loud cheer from the troops getting ready to load the plane. They had served their time . . . going home . . . might make it by Christmas. They were naturally elated to leave that place. Some of the guys going home were badly burned, some had missing limbs, and some were in wheelchairs.

Another shock I had received within just a few minutes of being "in country."

Someone blew a whistle and told us that we would be getting our unit assignments at about 0700 hours so we were to stay around the pavilion for the next four hours. He said, "Sleep, smoke, whatever; just don't go away."

Where would we go? We were scared to death with the sounds of artillery, mortars, and machine gun fire all around us. We didn't know the difference between outgoing or incoming!

I had learned to smoke in basic training. They occasionally would give us a ten-minute break and say, "Smoke if you got 'em." If not, they always seemed to find something for us to do. I was 19 and in the Army—time to learn to smoke. Several of us gathered in a corner of the pavilion and started talking and smoking. We were all lost, wondering what had happened to us. The smell seemed unbearable, even the cigarettes wouldn't cover it up. We watched them complete the loading of body bags. I wondered if that was the way they had sent my cousin home. It sure didn't seem very respectful. I had seen on television where the Vets came home in caskets draped with flags. I wondered lots of stuff about the guys in those body bags—about their lives, about their families, and about how long they had been over there before coming home like that.

I felt sick. I looked into the faces of the other guys and saw the same questions on their faces. How many of us would be loading a plane in a year still alive and with all of our body parts? Would we leave here in a body bag? We were tired, but there was no way to rest. So we smoked, talked, and waited until the 0700 hour.

As daylight came and we could see our surroundings, I was glad we had landed at night. How could any place be this dirty and disgusting? The air looked like smog, tin shacks were everywhere, and Vietnamese people were all around. *How can we tell whom we are supposed to help and whom we are supposed to shoot?*

In the area of the airport, they rode bicycles, motorcycles, and buses. We didn't have any idea that we were in one of the best places to be in country. We saw Air Force guys on the balconies of apartments with Vietnamese women . . . their uniforms hanging on the clothes lines. We knew, however, that we were in the Army, and things would be different for us.

Zero seven hundred hours finally came on the morning of December 24, 1967. An Army Sergeant started telling us to fall in and pay attention. My entire training class was there, plus several other groups of troops. He started reading off names and units: Artillery, Infantry, Armor, Aviation, and Engineers. He named every place I could think of someone could be going. I finally heard my name and 11th Armored Cavalry. Every unit had someone there to pick their guys up and take them to join their unit. *What is 11th Armored Cavalry?* What does that mean? I finally spotted one guy I knew. He just happened to be from Oklahoma too. I asked him what kind of unit we were going to . . . he had no idea . . .

There were about 20 of us standing there, and no one knew the Sergeant-in-charge. He said once again to pay attention. He gave us our squadron number. He said Mike and I were to be in the 1st Squadron—Tanks. All the other guys seemed to know what was happening to them, and they weren't surprised. All the men we had traveled with were going to Artillery or Engineering groups. I was still not doing anything but what they told me to do, never speaking up or drawing attention to myself, but this was just too much. I wasn't supposed to go to a tank unit. There had to be some mistake!

31

I raised my hand and the Sergeant said, "Yes, Hon, we'll eat when we get to your unit."

"No, Sergeant, I have survey training. There must be a mistake."

"Trooper, how long have you been in the man's Army?"

"Five months."

"Well, that's long enough to know the Army doesn't make mistakes. You'll be going with us."

"Sergeant, please double-check. I've never even seen a tank, except on television."

"You been to college?"

"Yes, Sir."

He said, "Well, it might take you a little longer, but you will be able to drive in no time!" I wasn't going to say another word!

In a few minutes, we loaded our duffel bags into a 2.5-ton truck, climbed into the back, and took off. The Sergeant said, "Take a good look at the city, boys. You'll be lucky to ever see it again." He gave us a little orientation to Vietnam (what we could hear over the rough ride and noise of the truck). The main topic was venereal diseases. We were all just riding, looking, and not realizing the kind of danger we were in by just going to our base camp . . . none of us with a weapon.

I saw nothing but filth, huts, oxen, and people. I had seen sandy soil before and driven roads with it a foot deep, but I had never seen dirt like this. It was deep and more like powder. The sweat rolled from us, and the red dirt just stuck to us. I could feel it going deep into my pores and into my lungs. An old memory came to me as I ate the dirt. My grandfather had once told me that every man would eat a bushel basket full of dirt in his lifetime. He had passed away years earlier, but I thought to myself . . . *Grandpa, I'm eating mine all at once.*

My eyes and throat were both burning. I think we traveled around twenty miles before reaching base camp. The sign read:

Black Horse,
Home of the 11th Armored Cavalry

We drove around the perimeter, and he dumped us off as we got to our units.

My feet hit the ground and dust flew everywhere. I was soaking wet from sweat. I was already one of the filthy ones. We went to the supply room, and the Sergeant said, "You guys hungry?"

"Yes."

"Go eat at Headquarters."

We asked, "Where's that?"

"About one-half mile straight south." Mike and I looked at each other. The Sergeant continued, "Yes, walk! We don't run a taxi service. Most guys are happy to get a hot meal." We walked, trying to look over the base camp. Headquarters looked as if it was mostly tents with very few permanently constructed buildings.

We arrived at the Mess Hall. The dust was choking us, and we were starving. I couldn't remember eating since the snacks we received on the commercial plane coming to this place. We walked into the Mess Hall and just saw more dirty guys looking at us. You can tell in a minute which ones are the new guys . . . they have shiny white skin and their eyes are bright with fear. Wrapped Christmas presents were on a table by the door. We went through the line and got our Christmas Eve meal. Most of the other guys seemed to enjoy it, but it didn't seem very special to me. I was just there . . . still numb.

As we left, someone yelled for us to take one of the presents. I remembered thinking . . . *there are guys here that really might enjoy a gift.* I didn't take one. Besides, I had already had my Christmas early back home with my family.

We walked back to the 1st Squadron Headquarters looking for the Sergeant who sent us to eat. We found him in a supply hooch. He said, "Come in and pick out your weapons." I looked over at a pile of M-16s. They were dirty, the stocks on them were broken, and the straps were either missing or broken. Some were even bent and most still had dried blood on them.

How much more of this can I take? It seemed like they were putting more on me than I could stand, but what was I going to do?

The Sergeant told us not to get an M-15 or an old M-16 because they would jam. I looked at Mike. I knew neither of us knew what he was talking about. I tried to ask one of the other new guys what to get and he said, "The Sergeant just told you!"

"I heard him, but I don't know the difference," I replied to him.

He yelled it out, "You don't know the difference?"

"I've never shot an M-16. I don't know how to take it apart or clean it."

He said, "Where are you from . . . Arkansas?"

"No, Oklahoma."

"How 'bout you?" he asked Mike.

Mike answered, "Oklahoma."

"We got some Okies out in the field, but they know what an M-16 rifle looks like!" The Sergeant ran through the stack of M-16s and handed us both one. I told him the strap was broken on the one he gave me.

"Hon, take the strap off another one and put it on that one, okay?"

"Yes, Sergeant," I answered.

He asked, "Do any of you other new guys know how to clean your weapons?" They all raised their hands. "Well, please take one of these two and show them how."

A guy from Tennessee helped me, and I thanked him. He was very patient and nice to me. He could tell I really needed help and he said, "You know I been in the Army five months, but I know about an M-16! How come you don't?" I explained to him that I was trained in survey and map reading.

"And you joined for an extra year to get that training? Here we are, both of us, same place, only I'll get out a year earlier."

He said, "Who's going to win the game?" OU was playing Tennessee on New Year's Day. I was and still am a big OU fan so we made a dollar bet.

Later on that day, the Sergeant came by and told us to come and get our jungle boots and jungle fatigues. Jungle boots had a metal plate in them in the sole to provide some protection from landmines and bamboo sticks placed by the Vietcong. They were vented on the sides to help prevent jungle rot. The fatigues fit looser and were made of lighter material to help us stay cooler in the jungle heat. We had flak jackets, steel pot helmets, canteens, ammo, and pills, pills, pills . . . for malaria . . . to make the water drinkable.

I got into my cooler clothes as soon as I could. My cigarettes were ruined from the sweat. One of the guys told me a soap holder would keep them dry. I looked around me and saw large metal chunks lying around our hooch and supply area. The mail clerk told me they been mortared the night before, but no one was killed. He said there weren't very many soldiers there.

The sweat had already started to run down my legs. I had dyed green underwear. The dye was starting to come out and was beginning to gall me. I saw the showers down the hill a few yards away. I decided to shower off. The large water barrels were on the roof. The sun warmed the water. I pulled a chain to receive my limited 3 gallons of water.

The outhouse consisted of several seats of wood with half-metal barrels under them. They were pulled out daily. Diesel oil was poured in them and burned. That was really a 'crap' detail. Another smell that was different from anything I could have imagined. Two days in country. Everything was unbelievable. I thought the world had ended. *How did I get here?* If I made it, I only had 363 days left. Tomorrow was Christmas Day.

The Sergeant told us we probably wouldn't go to the

field until the next day, so we're to use our time getting our stuff ready and write Mama to tell her how great we were doing. Almost everyone had been drafted. Only a few of us had enlisted. I thought of how many guys from basic had taken Air Borne Green Beret Training. They were still going through training and at least learning what an M-16 was or something that might save their lives!

On Christmas Day the Sergeant said, "I need to talk to you and Mike." We went up to the 1st Sergeant's office. He began to tell us how lucky we were to be members of the 11th Armored Cavalry. He, of course, laughed saying they had gotten a couple of map boys every six months or so. "We don't have to teach them to read maps, plot targets, or call in artillery. We use you college boys for Forward Observers. Some officers we get can't do that. But first, you'll get used to the field. We'll make you APC Drivers." I found out later that was an Armored Personnel Carrier. I didn't ask him. I was already the talk of the camp, and to think, I had spent my first five months just trying to fade into the woodwork!

The 1st Sergeant told us that if the APC ran over a land-mine, the driver was usually the only one we would lose. If it was a new guy, he didn't have so long to suffer through this place. He told Mike that he'd probably go to FDC (Fire Direction Control). They would take the coordinates and estimate the powder charge, the elevation, and the azimuth for the 155 self-propelled Howitzers, in order to hit the target from whatever position they happened to be in. They traveled as the squadron did, with the Howitzer Battery.

He said to me, "You'll be a driver. We need you to go with the tanks and APCs. You will learn to be a radio operator on Ambush Patrol." Ambush Patrol . . . that word hit me hard. I remembered my cousin had been killed while on Ambush Patrol, along with his entire platoon. I had the biggest knot in my throat.

I did my best just to answer, "Yes, 1st Sergeant." He

asked us if we wrote to Mama and if we had all our things ready to be choppered to our unit in the field.

He said, "It may be tomorrow . . . December 26th."

We didn't know what day it was over there; we just kept track of the number of days we had left in Vietnam. "I've not spent one day in the field and don't plan on going," the 1st Sergeant said. That's when being a 1st Sergeant came in handy. He had choices, but naturally, we had none. He told us to make a trip to the PX if we needed cigarettes, toothpaste, or anything else. I got a soap dish for my cigarettes and a good lighter (which I still have). They had some neat stuff. All the people working there were Vietnamese. They lived off the Base Camp in a village nearby. I couldn't help but wonder about their loyalty to the U.S. I already had my pens and paper to write home, and the postage was free. On Christmas Day, I organized my things and wrote to my future wife and some of my relatives that were truly concerned for me.

I was saved and baptized at a young age. I had several pins for not missing Sunday School, and I knew all of my relatives were praying for me. My mother had put a New Testament in my duffel bag before I left.

I didn't know much. I didn't want to know much. In two days I had seen and felt so much misery. I couldn't find much good to say about God and had little understanding of what was happening to me. I just felt that God wasn't a part of my life at that time. God is Love. I knew He was with me, but I didn't know where or how to call on Him.

CHAPTER 3
GOING TO THE JUNGLE

"The cords of death entangle me; the torrents of destruction overwhelmed me. The cords of the grave coiled around me; the snares of death confronted me." Psalms 18:4–5

Early the next morning we packed our things, and we were taken by the Supply Sergeant to the LZ (Landing Zone). We loaded into a Chinook chopper to go to our units. They loaded several supplies and hooked a large net on the bottom, full of 155 howitzer ammunition. The long blades started turning and dirt started flying, and we could feel static electricity, along with tremendous vibration. As we lifted up out of the dust, we shook, and it was so loud we could not hear ourselves think. I could look down through the cargo hole in the floor and see the net of ammo hanging below. We didn't know what to expect. I kept wondering about enemy fire or the Chinook going down. I saw some of the terrain. It looked like mostly jungle, some squares that may have been rice paddies, some huts with tin roofs shining, and some grass. It didn't seem to take very long. We landed in another storm of dust and dirt. The cargo Sergeant told us to move quickly so they could leave. So mailbags were loaded, a couple of troopers boarded, and they were off again.

It looked like some sort of camp was set up with tanks and APCs forming a circle. The 155 Howitzers were in the middle. A Mess Tent and Headquarters were set up. The Squadron

Commander was a Lt. Colonel. My Troop Commander was a Captain. There were several 1st and 2nd Lieutenants; most of them had been drafted. Everyone seemed easy to get along with. We reported to a First Lieutenant Executive Officer (XO). He told each one of us where to take our things and where to report. A Troop, B Troop, C Troop, D Troop, Howitzer Battery, and Headquarters were all needing men. He sent Mike to Howitzer Battery to FDC, just what First Sergeant had told him. He told me he had two map readers in Headquarters' tent, and they'd show me where to put my stuff on the APC in B Troop. "For a while, you'll be there. Sgt. James will welcome you to B Troop."

What a welcome I got as I was walking in the direction of B Troop! I walked in front of a 155 Howitzer. They had just begun shooting a fire mission. The muzzle blast almost knocked me down. The dirt surrounded the 155 Howitzer. I couldn't hear anything; I thought for an instant it was over. My third day. My suffering was done. I could see someone moving his arms and yelling for me (the new guy) to come over there!

It was Sgt. James from B Troop. He was a Sergeant E-7, a big, burly guy with a handle-bar moustache. He was calling me eighteen kinds of stupid and saying something about a fire mission! He pointed to my ears so I stuck my finger in one of them and found that my ear was bleeding. I had burst my eardrum. He put something in it that burned so badly it made tears come to my eyes. He said, "Huh! Must have a hole in it!" I still couldn't hear very well, and it still hurt.

He pointed to an APC and told me to put my stuff over there. He said they were two men short. Sgt. James said, "You'll be the driver!"

So I went through the same story, "I've never even been in one."

He said, "Jesus, son. It has a steering wheel cut in half. You turn left, it goes left. Turn right, it goes right. The other lever says D & R. I think a college boy can figure that one out! One more thing, Troop. You throw a track; you put it back on!"

I didn't say nothin.' One of the guys that was on the APC gave me some cotton for my ears. It helped to stop the air from going into my eardrum. Three days . . . the day after Christmas. *I'm glad I have a big family praying for me, because it's going to take all of them.*

In a few minutes, two guys walked up to me and said they were Forward Observers. They said there weren't too many of them around, and they'd help me out and teach me the ropes. We did become very close—some of the few whose names I knew. They were from Wyoming and North Carolina—Chris and Ronnie. Ronnie had about nine months left in country, and Chris only had six months. They took me to the area where they plotted targets of suspected enemy locations. I said, "This is the first thing since I've been here that I know how to do." They laughed and told me they were the same way. After three weeks, I'd be an old-timer ready to go!

They said, "Sgt. James is tough. He has a hard job. He is short (not much time left) in Vietnam and short in the Army. He had 21 or 22 years in the service, so he didn't want a bunch of guys around him that didn't know anything. If you need him, he's there. You may go with him tomorrow. We are in a hot zone (very dangerous, lots of enemy troops)."

They told us a mess tent was set up before Christmas, so we'd have a hot meal. Chris said, "I'll come get you at mess time unless something is going on." He came and got me—what they thought was a treat didn't do too much for me—but I ate everything they gave me.

When night fell, I didn't know what to expect. The two guys in the APC told me not to worry about sporadic fire. They said they'd take care of it tonight, and they told me to just try and rest while I could. They said we had four ambush patrols out, and at different times during the night, each troop would shoot sporadic fire, plus some of the 155 Howitzers would fire.

When Rex started shooting the 50-caliber machine gun in sporadic fire, it scared me to death. The brass landing in the floor was red hot. I kept moving so it wouldn't hit me. I wondered how in the world you could ever rest or sleep in this place. I may have gotten two or three hours off and on. It seemed like machine gun fire was constant. As daylight rose again on my fourth day, the first face I saw belonged to Sgt. James.

He said, "Get ready, we need to check on our ambush patrol. They got hit hard last night." I got what I thought I needed. About fifteen of us went in the direction of the patrol. Sgt. James took a medic and some ponchos. He said we were out of body bags so we were to grab our ponchos. We walked about a mile. It was my first time to see what the jungle looked like. I couldn't believe it! I didn't see how it could be any hotter! I couldn't breathe; it was dense and steamy. I was soaked as I wore my flak jacket, a heavy vest supposed to stop a bullet or shrapnel. It weighed about 15 pounds.

The Ambush Patrol had reported receiving heavy fire and some mortars. I didn't know what to expect. No one was talking, and they were being as careful as they could be. I could not have been more unprepared for what I saw as we approached the patrol site.

We lay down and started crawling up to their position. Body parts were scattered. The Vietcong were lying all over the place. First combat . . . dead. I could see the patrol of B Troop had been hit by a mortar. They were everywhere. We checked all the VC to make sure they were dead. I was scared to death. If someone moved, we were supposed to shoot and take his weapon. The sun was beginning to swell their bodies. Sgt. James said the rice they ate made them swell quickly.

We placed our ponchos on the ground and began trying to gather up our troops. We were told to match the body parts up as well as we could. I could not handle the sight, the heat, and the fear. I was just plain scared to death, and I began throwing up. It seemed like forever.

Sgt. James said, "Can you make any more noise? I would like to get home. We lose more guys than we can replace. When new guys come, I get a college-boy map reader! Those guys haven't even been messed with!" I didn't even want to know what that meant.

We carried our ponchos back and had to drag some of them. I was so sick, tired, and soaking wet. It took forever to get back. Some more medics and a doctor came and took over. They called in a chopper to take them out. Sgt. James came over and told me to go wash my face at the water trailer, wet my head, and relax. "You'll get use to it. I'm just sick of this place. I have a wife and four kids. I don't have anything personal against you. This is one place we all have to work together. Don't you wonder why you didn't stay in college?"

I replied, "Sgt. James, I wonder a bunch of things . . . like how are the next 361 days going to go for me?"

"If you see 361 more days, it will be great. One of the guys we picked up today had three days left. He should never have been out there. We are just short on men," he replied.

I sat under a shade made by a trailer, and I looked up to see Chris coming. He said, "We all had to do that for two or three weeks. After that, we didn't mind doing anything else they asked us to do."

I replied, "Chris, I already don't care . . . three weeks of seeing and doing this!"

"We don't lose guys every night," he said," so just pray for our guys." He told me the story again of the sergeant only having three days left, but he told me more about himself. He was married and had a baby girl he had never seen.

I just prayed, "God, don't let that happen to me. Take me out of here now."

Chris asked me if I had written home yet, and I told him I had. He told me not to write about this stuff because it is harder on our families than we know. He said to always tell them I'm doing fine. I told him that I knew that . . . so this is the first time ever to write most of this.

As bad as it was, I was glad Sgt. James and Chris acted

human toward me. I was always good at "sucking it up" and doing whatever I had to do, but right now, I was feeling pretty sorry for myself. I could see no way out, and I had only been there for four days. I had absolutely nothing to look forward to . . . still hadn't shot my M-16 that someone else had put together for me. I wondered if it would jam when I would have to shoot someone. I just felt like the whole world had dumped on me. I knew this was just the beginning.

I remembered something my grandmother (whom I was very close to) told me. She said, "God will not put more on you than you can stand." At that point, I had already started wondering if God was there at all.

We got word that we would be moving locations the next morning. I ate at the mess tent that evening, then went to the medic. I still had the cotton in my ear, and I knew it was dirty. He took it out and rinsed my ear, put clean cotton back in my ear, and gave me some antibiotics to take to keep my ear from becoming infected.

As night came, only one patrol went out. It wasn't us. It seemed like a quiet night, or I was just so tired that I was learning to sleep through it. I was dirty when I woke up; my clothes were stuck to me. I was really starting to get galled. I took my boots off to put on clean socks. I was getting blisters from the new boots; however, that stuff didn't really seem to matter much. I was anxious about the move, and I didn't know how that was going to take place.

Sgt. James came by and told me to check the oil and fuel in my APC. He said to just follow everyone else. He told us that we couldn't get lost. We were only going about three miles. Everyone said it would be an easy move, even closer to Base Camp. They had been in the field for 2 1/2 months and felt like it may be their turn to return for a week or so. We made the move drawing no fire and started to set up camp.

The two guys I was with were really great. One was from Chicago and had seven brothers and sisters, but he hardly ever got a letter. He had eight months left. The Tank Commander, Sgt. E-5, was from Georgia, and he only had six months left. He talked to me through the headsets and helped me with the driving. However, it was as they told me. It wasn't hard, even for a college boy.

Rex, the guy from Georgia, had handed me a box of C-rations and said all the good ones were gone. I got some kind of chicken noodle. I noticed the date on the box . . . 1943. I said, "This stuff is WW II rations, ya'll!"

"They changed the crackers; they're only two or three years old. Just be glad you got 'em," they laughed.

The APCs and tanks formed a large circle for the perimeter. The Mess Tent, Headquarters, 3 APCs with large canvas extensions, and the FDC tent were all tied together inside the tanks. The 155 SP Howitzers were inside the circle with tents set up for the troops that manned them. The Mechanics' tent, the first-aid tent, the mortar units, the tanks with dozer blades, and the flame throwers were all there. We had enough equipment to do just about anything. I met a guy from Oklahoma that was a mechanic. There weren't very many of them. They worked all the time; there were plenty of things to fix. I'm sure when they were sent to Vietnam that they hoped to be in a Base Camp Motor Pool somewhere, not in a traveling tank unit always in the field.

I finished eating and saw Chris. He wanted me to go to Headquarters with him. They were going to plot the night's target. He said they had planned again for four Ambush Patrols and a lot of sporadic fire. We plotted what we thought would be enemy activity. He called the coordinates to the FDC (Fire Direction Control), where Mike was. I had seen him once since we got there. They had two tents set up with the Howitzer Battery, and they had to relay the information to the Howitzer when a fire mission was called.

It was starting to get dark so I went back to my APC. The guys there told me to sleep if I could. They would man the

50-caliber machine gun. The move had tired me. There are no soft places on an APC or tank; it was all just metal. My back was sore from just the short trip, but as each day was passing, I was getting more tired so sleeping was easier, no matter the conditions.

I slept for a few hours, and it seemed like everything began happening at once. Rex was firing the 50-caliber machine gun, and Joe was firing one of the M60s. It sounded like they were both telling me at once to man the other 60-caliber machine gun. The long magazine of ammo was already loaded, so all I had to do was pull the trigger. The entire perimeter was firing, APCs, tanks, and mortars. It was dark-dark; you couldn't see anything. Everything was fully automatic, and every fifth round was a red tracer. I didn't know if we were being overrun. I knew we were being mortared and to keep shooting until someone told me to stop. Hot brass was covering the floor, and it seemed like we shot forever.

When it finally ended, we could hear that the ambush patrols were in trouble. They needed artillery support, which they received as fast as the Howitzers could be loaded. After heavy artillery support for over an hour, we had no contact with two of our patrols. The other two had lost two or three men apiece and had some wounded. About all that could be done was to wait until morning. There was no more sleeping for any of us the rest of the night.

As morning came, I could not believe my eyes. There were dead Vietcong inside our perimeter, hand grenades that had not gone off, bodies lying all over, and mortar shrapnel everywhere. Some of our mortar men had been injured, but no one killed inside the perimeter.

Sgt. James came, telling us to check out the Ambush Patrols. He sent three APCs for each patrol. Rex told me that was unusual so be ready; he told me to wear my flak jacket and steel pot. "You'll have to drive, but I don't think we will have to be first. If we get hit, turn into the fire, come back here, and man the other 60-caliber machine gun." We, like almost every-one else, were short a man; some were short two men. I couldn't help but wonder where the troops were that President Johnson had called for in record numbers. It seemed like we needed some of them. I thought even college boys would work!

We began to move toward the patrol that we hadn't heard from. I didn't have any idea what we might see or get into. Sgt. James told us to shoot if somebody moved, making sure they are not "friendly" (on our side). He then said, "However, I don't expect to find any." I got sick again, but I didn't throw up. I was just hoping I'd be able to face what I might see . . . my fifth day. We saw what I could only try to explain—a war-torn jungle, Vietcong dead, and some blood trails where they drug them-selves off or someone else drug them.

We got to the patrol site. I remember to this day saying, "Oh, Jesus . . . ," not calling on Him. I didn't know to do that; I was just saying His name. They were all dead. We could see that the claymore mines they had set around the perimeter had killed some Vietcong, but most of them had been turned around so that they fired back at the patrol. Mortars and hand grenades were all around them. We, again, started moving them and putting them in ponchos. I wondered how long the ponchos would last at this rate. Joe and I were standing together in the middle of them. My throwing up was over.

Then, somebody beside us moved. I got so scared the hair on my neck stood up. Then one of our troops spoke to us. He was alive! He had pulled two dead bodies over him. He had shrapnel in his legs and had lost a lot of blood. I'll never forget the look on his face. He said, "I'm sorry, I'm sorry, They ran over us, stuck the guns in our backs to make sure everyone was dead. I covered myself with my buddies so they would think I was dead. I'm sorry. I did all I could do."

Sgt. James came quickly to his side, "We know the kind of trooper you are. Son, in your place, we would have all done the same thing. I'll get you to the medic and get you evacuated out of here." We completed picking up bodies. Then we went on a Search and Destroy mission. We looked for VC, weapons, or anything they might have left or might still be hiding. We found a few bunkers and threw hand grenades into them before searching.

I looked at Joe and asked, "Am I going to have to go in there?"

He said, "Some day, yeah, but I'll do it today." Joe was smaller than I was, and I guess he had done it a lot of times. Joe looked somewhat Asian. He said in Chicago that there were some rough places. Sometimes just walking home from school was very scary. Yet after Vietnam, he just didn't care about anything. We continued searching several bunkers, only finding a dead Vietcong. The sergeant told us to take his weapon and ammo, and he told us to check and see if he had any papers on him, and then leave him.

As we walked off, Joe threw another hand grenade into the tunnel, scaring all of us. Joe said, "That felt good." We finally started back to our camp after almost an entire day. I was hungry and tired. We got back and opened up some more C-rations.

We heard that several guys had been killed in our other patrols. Sgt. James said he would need more men. I heard him saying, "Why we send these guys out there, I don't know. What does it accomplish? What does it possibly gain?" I listened to him and wondered the same thing. Sgt. James's toughness was gone for a few minutes. It had gotten to him. He knew all the guys that died, and it was really bothering him. I was thankful someone was acting human!

Sgt. James began to talk to me like in a fatherly way. He said, "It doesn't matter where you come from or what your training is as long as you stand up for each other. You stood up today. I'm proud to have you." He told me, "You just can't be over here and try to have understanding." He said your heart has to be hard; everything just has to be automatic. "You do it or you don't make it! After a couple of weeks, you will be so hard that you'll do anything; you won't care, and you won't even think of going home. You just have too much time to go."

He said I might even pray to die. He told me that Sgt. Williams will probably feel guilty the rest of his life because he didn't die, and his buddies did. He said he may never overcome the guilt. "When you get "short" like I am (less than 30 days to go), you get dangerous because your thoughts are of getting out of here. You start thinking you might actually make it; you let stuff get to ya.' You know you are losing too many good men, and you can't understand it." He continued, "We are losing this war, but the military is not running it. Politicians are. Westmoreland is being embarrassed as a General because of Johnson. He is not the idiot most people think he is."

He said that in a day or so we would be moving from that area and giving it right back to the Vietcong, and he was glad he didn't have to tell the mothers and wives of those men why they died . . . even though they died doing what our government asked of them, and they gave all they had. Speaking of mothers, he told me, "Write yours tonight. She needs to hear from you often. Just always tell her you're okay. It serves no purpose to feel sorry for yourself and make her live what you are experiencing." He continued, "Eat and get some rest; I'll tell Chris to leave you alone tonight. He can plot the target. I just hope our Captain is smart enough not to send patrols out. We are going to beef up our perimeter."

"Thanks, Sgt." I really appreciated his talk with me. I began eating my C-Rations and started thinking about my life. I was there . . . couldn't leave, except injured or dead. My heart was already getting hard and full of hate for the enemy. It hadn't bothered me for Joe to blow up a dead Vietcong.

I may or may not have killed my first man. I couldn't see while shooting my M-60 machine gun. I just knew that I hoped that I had. They didn't seem human to me—just the enemy, mean and evil. I tried to write home, but I couldn't think of much good to write about. My mind was going in a thousand different directions. I had never known hard and cold men before. A lot of these guys were younger than I was, but they were men. I had turned 20 in November. Was I to be a hard-hearted man, a warrior, and a brother to all the troops? If I was, my heart had to be hard and full of hate for the enemy. I really didn't know how to be like that, but I was learning quickly.

I wondered how one could change back to the person he was before the war. I knew a person couldn't live with hate or a hard heart, or could he? Would I just be crazy? I had seen and done more in five days than most people see or do in a lifetime.

I was really tired. I went to the medic, and he took the cotton out of my ear and put salve in it. He told me it looked good. I knew I was beginning to hear out of it again. I was so dirty. Everything stunk and was stuck together. I changed my socks and brushed my teeth. I asked Joe and Rex about a shower. They just laughed and said we'd take one in three weeks or so when we returned to Base Camp.

I had blisters and was galled. The medic had given me a salve for it, and it really burned. Joe told me I'd have to quit wearing underwear, or I'd never get well. He told me none of the old guys wear them. I just couldn't see myself not wearing underwear and decided to have my mother send me some on a pretty regular basis. It wasn't long, however, until I quit wearing them. I also took my boots off to sleep. My feet needed air. I knew if we started shooting, my feet would be burned by hot brass, but I just didn't care right then.

The next morning, after a mostly peaceful night, we were told we would move again . . . just a few miles . . . seemed like an awful lot of trouble to me. I had slept pretty well, but I could see how tired most of the guys were. They had been in the field for ten or eleven weeks. Their eyes showed their hopelessness. The only thing that seemed to lift their spirits was the thought of returning to base camp . . . or, even seeing someone like me, who still had 360 days left. They had considerably less time remaining. I could also see that killing or making the enemy suffer had begun to give them great pleasure.

A trip to base camp sure sounded good to me—clean clothes, a shower. We loaded up again and traveled a short distance. We went through a small village. There were huts, kids running beside us begging for food, water buffalo and carts, and a few small motorcycles. Off in the distance, maybe 75 yards, I saw 20 or more Vietnamese wearing black pajamas with red handkerchiefs.

I talked to my Tank Commander, Rex, over our headsets. I said, "Don't we shoot those guys?"

He replied, "No, they are supposedly South Vietnamese Rangers. That's why they are wearing those red scarves. That's all they have to do. They're not running so I guess they are South Vietnamese. Anyway, we can't shoot in a village, even if we draw fire. We can't chance killing civilians."

I asked, "Who is supposed to tell me these things? I guess I don't know anything!"

"You'll learn as we go, like the rest of us. Just don't shoot a civilian."

We arrived at our new location, and it was almost dark. Our Squadron Commander, a Lieutenant Colonel, flew above us in his chopper, getting us in proper position. The darkness began to overtake us so he landed, and we completed setting up, with lights used sparingly. It was an eerie feeling to turn on a flashlight when the enemy was out there and could shoot at the light.

We got set up and had another quiet night—only sent out one Ambush Patrol. They had no contact. I had to pull perimeter watch duty for two hours but slept pretty well. In the morning, the Mess Tent was going to set up for a hot lunch. They flew in a trailer with nonpotable water. It set in the hot sun for a while. Rex and Joe got a canvas bucket out of the APC that had a screw-on shower spout. Rex filled it up with water and hung it on a tent pole. He asked, "You got any soap?"

I answered, "Yeah, I got some, but didn't think I'd get to use it!"

He replied, "You're next after me and Joe." Rex turned the showerhead to get himself wet, then soaped up and rinsed off with about 2.5 gallons of water. Joe did the same, and then it was my turn. I never thought a shower could feel so good, even if we did have very little water. I had clean socks and fatigues stuck in an ammo box. It felt so good to be clean. I brushed my teeth and almost felt like a human again. Rex said, "That doesn't happen very often."

We were already beginning to sweat through our clothes, but we felt so good. Sgt. James came over and told us that we would be moving in three days—this time all the way to Base Camp. All the guys cheered loudly as we heard that news!

Wow! A shower and now this news! Even though I had only been there a few days, I was excited and ready to go. Chris and Ronnie came over and talked to me about Base Camp. We talked to the Captain. He told us when we got to Base Camp we could start training. We would work 12 hour shifts—12 hours on, 12 hours off—and then start learning to decode coordinates and radio scrambling procedures.

Chris and Ronnie told me it would keep us off guard duty and other details. It was still all new to me. I really didn't understand most of what they meant. Rex and Joe said it might be good for us. They said we'd be short-handed for Ambush Patrols outside Base Camp perimeter.

After a couple of quiet days, I was walking by a tank, and the guy from Tennessee yelled at me. "Hey, Oklahoma, it's half-time. The score is Tennessee 19—Oklahoma 0."

I said, "Is today the day?"

He answered, "Yeah, you better get your dollar ready." He was getting the game on his military radio. I couldn't believe it!

Here I am . . . the end of the world. Everything is depressing and miserable, and now my Sooners are getting beat! I was really disappointed, but I had learned in the past few days that a ball game wasn't nearly as important to me as it used to be.

I wanted to stay at Tennessee's tank and listen, but I couldn't stand any more depressing news. Chris told me that if I wanted to listen to it, he could get it on one of his Headquarters' radios. I was worried about us getting into trouble, and he told me if a fire mission came in that we would turn it off. He dialed in the frequency, and the second half had just begun. The Sooners were scoring and scoring! I had some old-fashioned excitement going on! And what was the final score? Oklahoma 21—Tennessee 19. I couldn't find Tennessee's tank fast enough. He was really disgusted, but we both knew exactly where we were and how our lives had changed forever. It was fun for a while, though.

The next day we loaded up and headed for Base Camp. The place I had been only a few days before had looked altogether different then. Now I saw that we had tents, showers, lockers, mess halls of our own, and we didn't have to walk to Headquarters.

I got some water in an ammo can and washed my clothes. It was nice. How could a place so bad look so good? Chris told me they always say we will get to stay a month, but he said we never do. It was usually only about two weeks.

They were building hooches all around our area: slab floors, 2 X 4 frames, 1 X 4 louvered walls with screen wire, and a tin roof. Sgt. James walked through and asked if anyone had carpentry experience or had ever driven a nail before. No one spoke up. I had two years of Vocational Technical Carpentry Training in high school and had worked as a carpenter during the summers. I wasn't about to share that with him. I didn't want on a work detail. He looked at me and said, "If I could mess with you, I would, but you will be with the college boys working with the officers. Has anyone told you that?"

"Yes, Sgt. James. Chris did."

"I put in your papers for Specialist 4th or E-4."

"Thanks, but I just got promoted to E-3 about thirty days ago."

He told me it would take a month or so. "Just stick with me; you're already in the slot. Rank comes fast over here. Somebody gets killed, or they rotate home."

I thanked him again, and he reminded me that there would be a time when I wouldn't be happy to be promoted . . . at least not in Vietnam.

I started looking for Chris. He was already at Headquarters.

I had thought about the 12 on and 12 off, and it was really sounding good—sitting in Headquarters plotting targets, calling in artillery, learning to decode. The best part was going to be not having to carry a body bag or poncho and not having to pick up our guys in pieces. It made me wonder a thousand things about their lives at home. It was much easier to just be a tough guy and not let any emotions show. These guys needed me to stand up when they really needed me.

Chris had already headed to Headquarters. We were back at Base Camp, but the war didn't stop. Most of the same functions we did in the field had to be done. I went to talk to Chris, and he said he thought I should train with him six hours and work with Ronnie six hours for a couple of days. Then I would do it myself. I began answering radio transmissions from the field (our units and other units that needed artillery support). I was trying to learn radio procedures so all coordinates would be scrambled and decoded—learning locations of each unit in our range of fire and trying to make sure all villages were plotted, even if any South Vietnamese troops were on Ambush Patrol.

Everything had to be done exactly. There could be no mistakes. When coordinates of locations were called in, they were usually done by an operator who was under fire. Sometimes he had to repeat his location to us several times so we could be certain before calling a fire mission to FDC. Therefore, 155 Howitzers could be loaded with correct powder charges, elevations, azimuths, even the right type of shell and fuse. After my first 12-hour shift was over, I was a nervous wreck, even though everything I did was checked by Chris. I kept thinking that in two days I would be doing this by myself. It finally dawned on me how extremely tired I was. Some of my free time had to be used for sleep. It was three o'clock in the afternoon or fifteen hundred hours, and 120 degrees. Those conditions seemed to matter less and less to me. I could see that everyone was tired, disgusted, and the air of hopelessness was so thick that you could almost see it.

I would never get over feeling sorry for the married men and some even had children back home. How sick they were! They had to hang on and had to hope they would get out of there so they could see their children again. I fell into another category—the same one most of the others were in. Just do what you had to do . . . be hard . . . not caring . . . because we knew we would never leave that place except in body bags. I felt differently than I had ever felt in my life. Most of my feelings were mixed up, and I was trying to be distant to the ones I loved the most.

I didn't want them to know how it really was, and I didn't want them to feel what I felt. I wanted them to live their lives and not worry about me. All my thoughts were pretty confused. I was glad I didn't have to hang on to any hope for 350 more days. I would just do my job, and whatever was going to happen would happen.

I worked with Chris and Ronnie for two more days before I got my first 12-hour shift. I was plotting targets when my first fire mission came in. I remember the nervousness. *What am I doing?* I'm an E-3, only six months in the Army, and I am calling in artillery by myself—no officers to oversee—just me doing another job and worrying if the shells were going in the right directions.

Some nights were pretty calm. It gave me time to write to

my family. I was being really careful, trying to be upbeat. I knew it was very important to them to get my letters.

We had been in Base Camp ten days when we got word that we would be going back into the field, near the Cambodian Border. It was called the Iron Triangle. The 3rd Squadron had been there and had gotten hit pretty hard, lost several men, and were forced to come back to Base Camp, so our stay was going to be a short one. The mechanics were working hard trying to get all our vehicles in good running order. We were happy to get some more men—only a few came. All were going to the Howitzer guns. Some of the APC troops would be getting two or three guys; we needed twenty or more.

I'll never forget when Rex came to Headquarters to tell me we were getting a guy for our APC. He said, "He is big and from Harlem. Does that bother you?"

I asked, "Why should it? Where's Harlem?" He began to explain to me where Harlem was and that the new guy was black. I was just thinking how out of place I was. I didn't know anything about the world, and I was doing things most men had never done or ever would do.

Rex said that he would be with us for a while. It was okay with me. I wasn't raised to be prejudice. I remembered something my dad had taught me about four years earlier. My dad, one of his friends, and I had stopped at a Dairy Queen in a small town. We had been hauling hay. A black couple with two small children was in front of us in line. When their turn came to order, the owner of the place told them to go around to the back door. It seemed like we had stood in line for a long time, and we were hungry and thirsty. My dad told the guy if the black couple was not good enough to eat there, then we weren't either, so we walked off.

Over the years on television and other types of media coverage, there has been a type of discredit towards the black troops in Vietnam. I felt like I was in one of the worst situations I could have been put in, but I never looked at these men as black, or any color for that matter, just good men, and the ones I served with were very good men. They stood up and fought as hard as anyone did. My opinion was very high of the black troops I served with.

Shortly before leaving for the field again, a friend from my hometown came into our hooch. I couldn't believe it. He had graduated from college and was drafted the same time I was, along with another guy who lived just down the block. He was married with one son. He said, "I heard you were over here. I'm with K Troop of the 3rd Squadron. We just pulled in yesterday. Bob is in the 2nd Squadron, and he is a medic."

I couldn't believe it. I said, "You got drafted? You could've gone to Officer's Candidate School, but you went with the draft? I joined another year to get some kind of training, and six months later, here we all are—the same unit in Vietnam. What a deal! The Army knew exactly where we were going when we got drafted." I felt like the smartest guy in the world. I would have been right here no matter what I did, except now I was going to spend an extra year in the Army!

We visited a little while about home, and he told me some about where we were going. He had almost the same attitude as mine; it was not very optimistic. I was never able to see Bob at all. We were always in different places, and I only saw Larry that one time.

CHAPTER 4
THE IRON TRIANGLE

They did not ask, "Where is the Lord, who brought us up out of Egypt and led us through the barren wilderness, through a land of deserts and rifts, a land of drought and darkness, a land where no one travels and no one lives?" Jeremiah 2:6

We loaded up again, ready for the field. Sgt. James came over to me saying, "You'll be the driver. We are going to the Iron Triangle near or next to the Cambodian Border." He continued, "I need someone with experience to drive. Rex will be the Tank Commander—Joe the M-60 gunner along with Harlem."

I laughed and said to Sgt. James, "I've been here four weeks, and I'm the one with experience? Are you going?" He told me he was going because he had no replacement, and the Captain told him he needed to go at least for two weeks. I said, "Sgt. James, no one could ever take your place, but I don't even see any E-6's around here, much less an E-7."

"You are getting to be an old hand and a smart aleck too!" He laughed, "A college boy 'Okie . . . somehow that don't mix." I informed him that I didn't graduate if that helped any.

I left early the next morning. I had already looked at the map, knowing it was a long trip, especially at 15 mph. The dust was relentless, and we couldn't see the tank in front of us, much less the one hundred or so total vehicles. We hit the trails at a slow pace. We were getting close to our location. I saw some abandoned vehicles on the side of the road, left there by the French in the 1940s or 1950s. *What a war-torn country we are in!* I sure couldn't see why we were fighting there; it was nothing but dirt and jungle. I didn't know anything about the history of Vietnam.

We were getting closer to Cambodia—going through what was enemy territory—commonly called Ho Chi Minh Trail. The going was rough and the terrain was more difficult to travel. The wheeled vehicles were having trouble and some had to be pulled. We ran into a large bunker complex. I was watching the bunkers and turned on a log, throwing the right track and disabling our APC. Rex got real upset, telling me never to turn like that. He said it was the driver's responsibility to put it back on. He knew I had no idea what to do.

We had a bad feeling about the area with all the bunkers, and now everyone was going around us. It was getting late, maybe two hours until nightfall. Sgt. James said after they reached what would be our camp area, he would send some mechanics back to help us. Rex asked for one or two APCs to provide us cover while we sat and waited. Sgt. James said we didn't have the people, and we'd be okay.

We all knew we were in a rough place. We felt it, and I knew we were extremely close to Cambodia. We were not supposed to be in Cambodia, but I did know how to read a map. Rex was still upset with me and that we had no help. He said, "This is a bad area. I don't like it that they left us here."

Just before dark, two APCs came driving up. The mechanic I had met from Oklahoma was driving one of them. One APC provided cover for us while we put the track back on. Harlem worked hard and helped us, not only because he knew what he was doing and had been trained on APCs and tanks, but also because he was so strong. I watched him duck down behind the M-60 shield so his head would not be above it. I don't remember his name. It was difficult to pronounce, so everyone just called him Harlem. He was a good man with a good heart.

I knew he hadn't seen everything . . . yet. I just hoped now wasn't the time. I knew it wouldn't take much to overrun us. We finally got it fixed and were back on the road to camp. It was dark. We drove as fast as we could to get there. We made it back and drew no fire. Rex and Joe thought that was it for us because the enemy was out there, all over the place, and yet they didn't take us out.

We took our position on the perimeter. Sgt. James came by and told us there wouldn't be an ambush patrol tonight. "We don't know what we have run into, but 3rd Squadron got kicked good. There are a lot of troops and a supply movement coming from Cambodia." We all knew Cambodia was being used as a supply route for the North Vietnamese. "We're going to set up sporadic fire and shoot mortars and 155 howitzers, but no ambush patrols," he instructed us.

For some reason, I decided to sleep on top of the APC, instead of in it. I was so dirty and hot and had grease all over me from the track, I just wanted to lie down. It seemed like I had just gotten to sleep when everything started happening all at once. We were getting mortared from every direction. It looked as if we were completely surrounded. I was trying to get inside the track before Rex and the rest of the guys started shooting back. It felt like I barely made it. We shot for hours. All the machine gun barrels were hot. We had to pour oil on them to keep them from warping. Pieces of mortars were hitting the sides of the APC. I knew some of the guys slept in tents. I just hoped they had had time to dig in. The mortar positions were too close to use our 155 howitzers. We had to rely on machine gun fire and our mortars. It wasn't too long until helicopter gun ships were coming in for support. Their M-60 machine gunners were firing rapid fire to help knock out some of the mortar positions. It was a very long and tiring night. I was so thankful we did not have any patrols out. We made it through with only a few minor injuries. We heard one of the chopper gunners got wounded, but we were never certain. Helicopter machine gunners' life expectancies weren't very long. Very few of them got home without getting many Purple Hearts or being in body bags. The Army, however, did give an extra fifty-five or sixty-five dollars a month for being one. We very seldom knew about them, even if they were assigned to the 11th Cav, unless they were shot down in the field. I had been there long enough to know they were a brave bunch of men. They did whatever they possibly could to protect and rescue men. They saw it all and did it all.

The morning finally came, and I already knew what to expect. I was talking to Harlem about what we would be doing. He acted as if he was prepared. He said his neighborhood wasn't a piece of cake. I looked around, and here came Sgt. James. He yelled, "Get ready. The brass is yelling for a body count. They think we got a bunch last night. They're just a few yards out there so we'll walk. There are no 'friendlies' out there, so shoot anything that moves!" He told me since I had learned so much about radio communication; I could carry the radio with my ammo, flak jacket, steel pot, and M-16. He told Harlem to get his 60-caliber machine gun unmounted from the APC so he could carry it with the ammo. He was so big and strong that he didn't seem to have any problem doing that.

It looked like the last time. Everything was shot up, trees downed, etc. The hot sun was glistening through some of the bamboo leaves. It was shining through the jungle like little silver stars . . . almost floating through the air. I wondered for a minute what was going on. There couldn't be anything pretty in this place. I felt as if God wasn't there. It didn't take me long to stop trying to find beauty in that mess. I was back to the fields of filth and death. We started counting bodies just about as soon as we started walking. Some were as close as 25 feet from our APC perimeter. It looked like a slaughter. There were some still alive as we began removing weapons and ammo from them. The body count was over 50 (some were men and some were women). We could see where some had been drug off into the jungle. I knew when Sgt. James saw the blood trails that we would be going in there.

After gathering up all the weapons and ammo, we crushed them with a large tank that was equipped with a blade for clearing and digging. Some of us grabbed an AK47, a great weapon the enemy had. It held more ammo than ours did, never jammed, and used their bullets as well as ours. Our weapons would not use theirs. They were made in China, as was most everything. A few were made in Russia.

Things just never ceased to amaze me. We got several thousand men killed because their weapons jammed before they got a better gun, and the VC still had a better and more dependable automatic weapon than we did. The track ran over the remaining weapons and ammo several times and then began digging a hole with the blade to bury the weapons. Sgt. James gave the order to dig it a little deeper, and then he told us to drag the bodies and body parts to the hole.

We started doing that when somebody moved. A trooper from C Troop unloaded his M-16 in direct fire . . . *made a mess*. Sgt James said we wanted them dead, but somebody had to pick them up, and it was us. Sgt. James said, "They are out there watching us, so to hurry and get it done." He told us we would be there for three or four more days.

Harlem asked, "Why are we burying them?"

"It's not out of respect, Troop. The smell is going to be awful." Harlem looked at me and said he was going to be sick. I told him to do what he needed to do; just two and a half weeks earlier, I had thrown up for an hour. In only a few weeks, I was the old guy, already hardened to some of what I was doing and seeing.

Harlem said, "My neighborhood is not like this. I can't handle it!" I told him to take his time, and I assured him he would be all right in a little while. It took us a couple of hours to get the job done. Sgt. James said we had a Sergeant that would burn them, but we were in a dark place. He could feel it. He said,

"I'm short, so just bury them." He continued, "Let's go back to the APC and get C-rations before we go into the area where the bodies were drug off."

"Let's eat!" Somehow that didn't sound like such a good idea to those of us who couldn't eat. We did need to rest. I headed for the water trailer to wash my hands and face. Harlem was already over there crawling around. I told him to stick his head under the faucet, and I'd turn it on for him. Just as I turned it off, I looked up and saw Sgt. James. I thought he was either going to give Harlem a little pep talk like he had given me or tell us we were going back into the jungle. Naturally, I was wrong again. He told me the water was not for showers. He told us to wash our hands and face and not to waste it. I told him that it was nonpotable water, and he raised his voice informing me that he knew what it was. We might have to drink it anyway. He said this area was so hot that we probably couldn't get a Chinook chopper in here with supplies. "So like I said, College Man, don't waste the water!"

Harlem looked at me and said, "Man, you are dirty. You've got grease, dirt, sweat, and blood all over you."

I looked him over and said, "If you weren't black, you'd look the same!" We both were able to manage a smile and sit in the shade for a while. Rex walked up and asked if we had eaten anything. We told him we weren't able to right then, and he informed us that we were getting ready to go on a Search and Destroy Mission. He said we were taking three tracks and two foot patrols. He looked at Harlem and told him if we took our APC, he would have to go. I didn't want Harlem to have to go, but I didn't want to have to walk either. We had moved all day the day before, had replaced a track, had to shoot under heavy fire all night, and had to spend all morning gathering bodies. I didn't think I could walk much more; I had so many blisters. I knew walking would be much more dangerous. The VC would know we were coming and would have booby traps set up everywhere.

Rex and Joe were at the APC. We walked over there as Joe was telling us it was time to go. He said the place doesn't look good, and we were taking four APCs, two tanks, and a foot patrol. "We won't have any artillery support because we're too close, and no one else can reach us. Chris is checking on some 8" guns north of us, but they were so far it was dangerous to try and use them."

We took off toward where the bodies had been drug off. I knew we were going into Cambodia, which wasn't very far away, and I also figured that's why we would not get any artillery support. We were not supposed to be over there at this point in the war. Any artillery damage to the terrain would probably cost our government lots of money. We found bunker after bunker—blood trail after blood trail. The more experienced guys told me that we were driving over tunnel complexes. "We're in deep stuff here," they said.

The foot troops were throwing grenades in every bunker, and some of them were entering the complexes. In only a few minutes, the tunnel complex had been found. We drug out all kinds of weapons and ammo. It was a large tunnel complex, and we knew we were not the only ones in it. The openings were very small and claustrophobic. When you broke through to the inner tunnels, they ran for miles. We blew up the part we had found and then left, not finding any dead or wounded. Nothing seemed right.

Rex said, "I can't believe we are not calling in air strikes to destroy this tunnel complex or at least the artillery."

"Rex, we are in Cambodia," I told him, then showed him on the map. I could see in his eyes that we were in trouble.

We left and went back to where our unit was and joined the perimeter. This time I ate what I could of my C-rations. I tried to doctor my feet; the blisters were gone, just raw meat. I went to the medic's tent to get something for them. He checked my ear again and said it was okay. I told him it felt fine. The medic said, "I'll get you the paperwork for your Purple Heart."

I asked, "What for?"

"Your ear!"

"I don't want that!"

He told me lots of officers had gotten them for ears. I told him I'd been here for 4 1/2 weeks and to give mine to some of those guys I've had to put in a poncho with their arms and legs gone! He said, "I agree. Most guys feel like you do."

He did give me something to help my feet. I got back to my APC. Most everyone was asleep. The last few days had drained us. I figured a couple of hours of sleep before nightfall would help, so I lay down on the ground beside the APC and slept.

Two or three hours later, Sgt. James came over and kicked my side saying, "Get up!" I tried, but my eyes had stuck together, and I had trouble getting them open. He said, "These idiots are sending out three patrols tonight, but at least they will be APC patrols, and not foot patrols."

I asked him if we were going, and he told me he didn't know yet, but to be ready just in case. Sgt. James said, "I got seven days left in this place . . . seven days in this man's Army . . . and I may have to go out tonight in one of the worst areas I've been in. We're still probably in Cambodia, and the Army won't admit it, and if I get Killed in Action (KIA) tonight . . . what a deal, man! I bet you wish you could get back over to Headquarters to plot targets."

"Sgt. James, it don't matter to me anymore. I'm so tired and dirty; how can it get any worse?"

"It will," he answered.

Rex came over and told Sgt. James that A and C Troops were going on patrol, not us. We almost hugged. I really did like Sgt. James and wanted him to get home to his family. I knew no choppers were going to come in and land, so I didn't know how they were going to get him out.

We did share time on night watch and perimeter fire, so we did get some sleep. About three o'clock A.M. the patrols broke loose. We monitored the radios and knew it wasn't good. They were getting hit with everything—mortars, machine guns, and RPG's. We could hear them calling for help and doing all they could. They sent more APCs to them, but mines had been placed everywhere. They were blowing up, killing the drivers, and disabling the APCs and tanks. Our mortars tried to help, but we knew they weren't doing much good. We couldn't do much. They had been put in a bad situation. Rex said that was so stupid. "You can't kill 50 Vietcong, bury them, destroy part of a tunnel network, and not expect to get hit! Those guys are doing all they can do."

I was doing my best to listen to Tennessee. He was the only one I knew. His APC was disabled by an RPG round, and they were receiving heavy machine gun fire. I could tell Tennessee had been hit, but was still shooting his M-60 machine gun. We had picked up several RPGs and ammo from the tunnels.

We found something that looked like a sawed-off shotgun; the barrel was about 12" long and made of bamboo held together with two radiator hose clamps. The metal trigger mechanism was made in China. They shot something like that at us, and it would go through an Armored Personnel Carrier, and in some cases, disable it.

Before long, we heard the roar of the choppers. They didn't know where to shoot, except when they were fired at. We had so many APCs strung out that they didn't want to shoot *friendly*. It was almost daybreak when things started to calm down. I knew we would have to go because we were still in one piece. We left at daybreak knowing we would see a mess.

Sgt. James told us to go in a straight line and go slow because they put mines everywhere. He told Rex to go first, which meant me because I was the driver. At that point, I didn't care. I drove as slowly as I could and ran over a mine after traveling just a few yards. I heard it click, and I backed up two feet or so—sweat was pouring off of me. Sgt. James determined it must be a dud and even made a joke about how tight my rear end was. I eased on forward, and the track behind me rolled in my tracks. The mine went off, blowing the driver all over the APC. They told me the guy was from a large coal mining family in Virginia.

It was an awful sight, and the track was disabled. His crew went to other APCs, and we continued to move toward our patrol. Rex kept telling me over the headset how lucky I was. He said, "Them people you got praying for you in Oklahoma must be doing a good job."

We got to the Patrol and were surprised to find that only two guys had been killed. Several were wounded. Tennessee was alive, but his left arm was gone below the elbow. They had put a tourniquet on it, but he was extremely weak. There was blood everywhere. They called for Medevac choppers, which always came, no matter the danger. The Captain told Sgt. James to get on one and go home. He didn't have a chance to say good-bye or even get all of his things, but he got out of there, and I was happy for him.

I knew Tennessee wouldn't be back. He'd go home, if he made it. I never even knew his name.

We lost four APCs and a tank, and as Sgt. James said, "All due to stupidity!" Our Captain came and told us a new Sergeant was on his way as soon as he could get there. He told us he was an E-7, Sergeant Taylor. He said he had been in the Army over 20 years, was new in country, but was a Korean War Veteran. We were all 19 or 20 years old, so he was in the Army before we were born. We couldn't wait for him to lead us.

We all wrote home when we got back because the mail was coming . . . water, supplies, and we figured, the new Sergeant. They were going to try and get a Chinook in to us. We heard it coming miles away and kept looking for it, hoping it would make it to us. It was loaded with a big net full of 155 Howitzer shells from underneath. There was no water trailer. It had supplies, and a big, fat Sergeant E-7 came down the ramp after it landed. He was lily white, bald-headed, and his boots were spit shined. He was directed to the Captain's tent and told to come to our area.

We were a filthy mess, and he was so clean. We could tell he was scared, but he wasn't going to admit it, which was okay. He looked older than my dad, and I guess he was. It was so hot, and he was really overweight. Rex laughed, "I don't think he'd make a good tunnel rat." He had his steel pot on with his chin-strap buckled, flak jacket on, and sweat was pouring down his face. He still had his old fatigues on, and they were drenched with sweat.

He asked us what our rank was and what we did. He said, "You need to wear your rank!" Nobody wore rank out there, not even the officers, but we said okay. He left to go put on his jungle fatigues. He looked like a big green Santa Clause. He wanted an AK47. We had several, so we gave him one.

We also had gathered up a few extra M-16s. I had one that was almost new, but I was still using my old one. What sleep I was getting was outside on the ground beside the track. I had my extra M-16 leaning beside me on the track.

I finally saw Chris and Ronnie. They had been busy. They told me we really had our hands tied in this area. There seemed to be two large VC movements along the Ho Chi Minh Trail. If we weren't in Cambodia, we could probably call in a B52 bomber. Ronnie told me he had been ready to go with A Troop last night as Forward Observer for them, but everything was too close. Those guys should have never been out there. I told them about Tennessee. They didn't know him. Chris asked, "Did you save his arm?"

"I threw it in the chopper." I told Chris I had gotten sick again, about the time I thought I could handle it.

I told them about our new Sergeant (Taylor) and about wearing our rank. They laughed and said, "He'll get over that. We get new ones that try to 'play Army,' and it just doesn't work over here. He'll learn."

Chris said something must have been happening somewhere. "We're not getting any help, and everyone seems to be talking about their New Year cease-fire, something they called Tet." I told them I didn't think those guys around us had gotten the word.

I asked them if we would be getting any more water. They said they doubted it because they had given us pills to purify our nonpotable water for our canteens. I said, "Great! I don't think I have ever been this dirty!" He told me four days wasn't very long and that there would be a time when I'd see thirty days without a shower.

That night we stayed on the perimeter. It was a dark and eerie night, but only sporadic fire was used. I think the brass finally saw that we needed to be on the defensive, instead of the offensive. During the sporadic fire, we shot 50-caliber and M-60 guns every couple of hours or so.

Someone from the inside of the perimeter was shooting a 50-caliber. It was so dark that you could not see anything. Rex said, "I think that is the XO's track (Executive Officer and 1st Lieutenant)." Sgt. Taylor was staying there after C Troop started complaining they were drawing fire from inside. It stopped. Rex and a C Troop sergeant found out who it was. It was Sgt. Taylor. He thought we were being attacked. He was lying down inside and had his shoes and socks off where the hot brass hit the floor. It started burning his feet, and as he came out, he had on nothing but his underwear. His feet were blistered, and his gut was hanging out. We laughed, and he got mad and said someone could have told him what was going on. Rex told him if he would have shot someone in C Troop, he would have learned in a hurry.

"What rank are you?" he had asked Rex.

"E-5 Sgt.," Rex answered.

"Well, I'm an E-7 Sgt. First Class, and you don't talk to me like that!"

"I could care less what rank you are, but I can tell you this . . . if you endanger our lives, you don't last long!"

"Are you threatening me?"

"I'm just telling you . . . you better listen to someone that knows what is going on, or you won't last long," Rex told him.

The Commanding Officer had told Sgt. Taylor he needed to let it go—*now!* He did.

The next morning I knew we were going to hear from Sgt. Taylor. He told Rex to start the APC and check out all fluid levels and grease the tracks. He told him to do all the maintenance, which was the driver's job, not the Tank Commander's. I was surprised, but Rex didn't say a word. He just did it. He moved the track back and forth a few times, still not saying anything. I was really shocked. Then I remembered my M-16! I had leaned it on the track earlier. He had run over it. I was carrying my original. This one came from one of the guys sent home in a body bag. I asked Rex what I was going to do with it. We laughed, and he said to throw it away. Unfortunately, Sgt. Taylor saw it and asked whose weapon it was. I told him I guessed it was mine, and he said, "I'll give it to the Supply Sergeant, and you can pay for it!" I told him he was crazy, and that I wasn't going to pay for anything. He said, "I'll make sure they take it out of your check, after they bust you to E-3."

"I am an E-3," I told him. "I send $150.00 per month home, and I collect $38.00 each month."

Rex took my arm and said, "Come on, let's go see Captain Holt and get this crap stopped now!" We did. Rex and Captain were pretty close. He was also from Georgia, a straight up guy, and he took no bull. Later he talked to Sgt. Taylor, and nothing was said to us again.

CHAPTER 5

TET

I pursued my enemies and crushed them; I did not turn back till they were destroyed. I crushed them completely, and they could not rise; they fell beneath my feet.
2 Samuel 22: 38–39

The Squadron Commander told all the officers and NCOs that a cease-fire had been agreed upon for the Vietnamese TET New Year celebration. We all knew that considering where we were, deep in the jungle, we could not trust that they wouldn't shoot us. However, the night was extremely quiet, and there was no sporadic fire. It was the darkest dark. You couldn't use lights or carry a flashlight, because you knew that would make you a sure target. There was absolutely no light. You could not see your hand in front of your face. We still maintained a guard on every APC, alternating every two hours. We couldn't help but wonder if the VC were doing anything or if they were sleeping. We were tired and just slept. It turned out that was the last night's sleep we would have for several days.

We got word that Saigon, our embassy, and Bien Hoa Air Base had been hit hard by regular Vietcong Army Troops. We had only seen VC in black silk pajama uniforms up to that point. We were ordered to Saigon. The 2nd Squadron was also on the way. It would take all day and most of the night to get there. It was a long trip.

We still had a very bad feeling. I knew the VC were still moving through, close to our location. Our trip could be shortened by several hours, maybe a day if a bridge could be built for us to cross a river using floating metal pontoon systems locked together. They were designed to carry tanks and equipment. The brass knew the urgency of getting us there as quickly as possible, so the Engineer Unit started to work on the bridge. Those guys' jobs were tough and hard, and they had to work with very little protection. The area was so hot a Special Forces Unit was called in with a battery of 105 Howitzers. We were en-route as fast as we could go. We were forced to leave all our disabled vehicles behind, which was very seldom ever done. We all knew the urgency in our getting to Saigon and Bien Hoa Air Base.

We were still several hours away from crossing the river. We kept hearing the engineers were being overrun. They were flown into an area as hot as ours, with little protection. We could hear the 105s blasting away for hours. It was dark, and we were doing our best to get there. As we went through a couple of small villages, we got orders to shoot if we drew fire. Rex said, "We could never shoot back. I've never heard of this!"

We got to the river as the sun rose. It was the worst site I had ever seen. There were enough bodies to cover a football field . . . all Vietcong . . . blown to pieces. They had gotten within twenty feet of the 105 howitzers. They were shooting direct fire beehive rounds. It was all they could do to keep from being completely overrun. I don't remember seeing a VC in one piece. There were body parts everywhere. It looked like a river of blood. We went by them as choppers were coming in to get the 105s and Special Forces troops. There weren't very many of them. We figured the dead and wounded had already been evacuated.

As we got closer to the bridge, we saw dead regular North Vietnamese Army Troops lying all over the edge of the road or trail we were using. They had regular camouflage fatigues, much like the Army wears now. The Engineers were sitting on their equipment waiting for us to cross. They looked terrible. As soon as we all crossed, except for C Troop who stayed behind to provide cover for them, they removed the bridge.

We continued toward Bien Hoa Air Base as fast as we could. Our Captain told us they had VC inside the perimeter of the air base. Saigon, the Embassy, had been taken. They were all over the city. We still had eight hours or so to get there.

We drew machine gun fire on the edge of a rubber plantation, another place we were not supposed to shoot, but that day we did. Some French villas were built by the French in the late '40s were overgrown with brush. They looked like homes on a southern plantation. You could tell at one time that they had been beautiful. Rubber trees were a big part of the Vietnamese economy. When we drew fire, we unloaded on them. If anybody moved, we shot and kept moving to Bien Hoa. We rolled in and shot and shot and shot. We blew buildings completely down, killing everything in sight. We had to shoot our way in. We knew the Air Force had some Army protection. It was a large complex. All we could do was shoot if they shot at us. We rounded up maybe 20 of the North Vietnamese troops alive and turned them over to the Air Force APs (Air Police). They were so scared. They thanked us a hundred times for helping them. They had never seen combat; I don't think they had ever even seen a Vietcong.

When C Troop caught up with us from protecting the engineers, they were told to go into the streets again for another sweep. Some of the 2nd Squadron had rolled into Saigon, killing hundreds of North Vietnamese. They were working with the Marines to regain control of the Embassy.

I had and still have great respect for the Marines. Their history of being warriors is surpassed by none, and my cousin had been one. My dad told me stories of WWII when he was a sailor, and he drove an LCVP (Landing Craft Vehicle Personnel) off the ship in the Pacific. He would let the Marines off on shore, and they would be slaughtered before they hit the beach. He said they just kept going. They were brave men who deserved to be honored. I learned, however, that no matter what branch of service you were in or what rank you held, in a time of war, you had to stand up and be a warrior.

In a couple of days, everything was beginning to quiet down, and the damage and losses were looked at. Our Unit had not lost one man. We were able to fight, and no matter how sick this may sound, it was fun for us to be turned loose and fight the way we were supposed to fight. We all knew if we could fight the way we were meant to, without all the restrictions, we could not have been stopped, but politics prevented that from happening. It caused us to be labeled as something we were not. We were warriors put into a situation that was a "no win" for us. We weren't allowed to win that war. The warriors didn't lose—the politicians did.

We set up our perimeter inside the Bien Hoa Air Base and looked around at the Air Force complex. They had metal buildings, electricity, EM Clubs, NCO Clubs, showers, stools that flushed, motor pools to work on vehicles, large tents set up for us to sleep in, cots with bedding, socks, fatigues, and a Mess Hall. We not only had hot food, but a choice of hot meals. What a deal! If my plans for the Air Force had worked out, I might have been in a place like this. It was great to shower, brush my teeth, put on clean clothes, and eat a hot meal.

We lay down in a tent with cots and slept great. Most of us took time to write home and say the best stuff we could, knowing the TET Offensive was so big it was in the papers and on the news. My uncle told me the 11th Armored Cavalry was on the front page of the Daily Oklahoman. It had a picture of us rolling into Saigon and Bien Hoa.

We had no guard duty, no patrol, no nothing; we just slept. The next morning, however, our holiday was over. Sgt. Taylor came in and told us we had to go into the streets of Bien Hoa and Saigon to gather bodies of VC. The Air Force was going to furnish us with 5-ton flat bed trucks. We were to load them. I had been in country 35 days. I had seen so much, done so much, and been sick so many times. I was learning so quickly to shut that out and try to be a strong trooper. Your heart had to be so hard, or you could not survive.

I thought I was over the hump until we went into the streets to pick up the dead North Vietnamese soldiers and VC, trying to distinguish them from the South Vietnamese that were dead and lying everywhere. The smell was intolerable. I tied a rag over my mouth and nose. There were children combing the bodies, getting what they could find from them. Some were sitting beside someone they loved and crying loudly—no one there to help them. The VC had killed hundreds of South Vietnamese civilians when they took over. Those kids really broke my heart. I couldn't stand to leave them there. We were all devastated.

The bodies were all swelling at a rapid rate and a few had burst open. The Air Force guys in the trucks had thrown up all over the place. We had to start loading the VC into the 5-ton trucks. We had a load piled up high, in a mound on the truck. We were taking them back to Bien Hoa Air Base. They had dug a tremendous hole to put them in. Our trucks did not have dump beds, but the Air Force trucks did. I was so thankful we didn't have to handle the bodies again. However, I saw some guys having to unload them by hand. The E-7 "Chief of Smoke" from the Howitzer Battery was in charge again. Unbelievable!

I asked Sgt. Taylor if they were planning to burn the bodies and he said, "I guess they have to!" I looked back at Sgt. Taylor. He looked really pale and just awful. Everyone was sick, but this looked like more than that. It was very hot, and he was so big. The "Chief of Smoke" started burning the bodies. The smell was awful, and I guess just too much for Sgt. Taylor. We put him in the truck and took him to First Aid. They had a nice facility and decided quickly that he had suffered a heart attack. Being where we were had saved his life.

We went back into the streets of Bien Hoa to gather more bodies. The children were still there. Harlem was still sick. We all were. The guys in the other trucks were going slow. It seemed the job was just so horrid. I think we made about 5 loads (around 500 bodies, I think). We dumped them into the burning pit. The smell clung to us. We went back to shower and threw our fatigues away. Our Lieutenant told us that Sgt. Taylor was going to Japan for surgery and then home. His military career was over. He said Sgt. Taylor said to thank us for getting him to treatment after the way he had treated us. Those things didn't matter. We were not full of hate for him because of a little Army "crap." The burn pit was on my mind, and the smell seemed to permeate the entire Base Camp.

Chris showed up and said his job had been taken over by the Bien Hoa Base Camp, and our guns would not be needed. "So," he continued, "they have a real neat NCO Club, bar tender, mixed drinks, big water cooled fans, a band—almost like the world."

I said, "But I'm not an NCO!"

"Keep your mouth shut, and no one knows. We don't wear rank."

I thought maybe this was what I needed—something to wash away my troubles. We drank too long and came back drunk, got on our cots, and slept all night. The next morning we wondered again what was happening. Sgt. Taylor was gone, and Sgt. James went home.

The Commanding Officer told us to hang loose. He said we might just sit around. He also put Rex in charge; Staff Sgt. E-6 would be given to him as soon as the paperwork went through. For now Joe would be made Tank Commander. He told us a new guy would drive Harlem and me. He said we would be M-60 machine gunners. The new guy was from Texas. He wanted to be called "Bear." I don't know why. He wasn't that big. He was always telling us what all he had done and where he had been. It really got on our nerves. Harlem told him he had lived in New York City all his life, and that he had been over there for three weeks. He said, "When you have been over here for three weeks, you tell me what all you have done, but until then, just shut up,

Bear!" The new guy told Rex he had driven an APC. We could tell right away that he didn't have a clue.

We all went to the EM Club. It got pretty wild. I was spending my $38.00 on .25 beers. We spent about a week there with nothing to do. We did too much drinking, and we started to wear out our welcome with the Air Force. All our vehicles were ready to go and in very good shape. All our weapons were cleaned and had been brought up to good condition. Rex came to me and said my E-4 papers were in the next pay period. I'd be E-4. I said, "Thanks!" I could tell Rex was not very excited about being E-6.

He said, "Having to choose who goes on patrol or who does what doesn't bring me much joy. I have all these guys' lives to think about. I shouldn't be in this position."

I was walking out of my tent and saw the Big Red One coming (the 1st Infantry Division). They were setting up across the street from us. I knew we would not be there much longer.

I heard someone calling my name. It was a guy who I had been in Ft. Sill with. He was surveying. I asked him if he was with The Big Red One. He replied, "No, I'm stationed here with the Air Force. I'm surveying a place for them to set up." He asked me how I had gotten in the 11th Armored Cavalry.

"Just the way it goes, I guess." I told him Mike was in FDC in my Unit, but I didn't see him much. He told me a couple of guys who were with him, and we talked about the Dallas Cowboys for a while. He was from Dallas, but was nothing like Bear seemed to be. He had to get back to work so I left.

Later that day, we got word that we would be moving again, going north. We had gotten use to the Air Base and hated to leave. We folded our cots and bedding, and put them in our APCs. We didn't ask anyone, but we really liked the cots. We started heading north. We had to travel the streets of Bien Hoa. It was still an awful sight. We threw out C-rations to the children as they ran beside us begging for them. Bear was jerking us all over the road trying to get used to the track and learning what he said he already knew.

CHAPTER 6
AMBUSH PATROL

Lift up a banner against the walls of Babylon! Reinforce the guard, station the watchmen, prepare an ambush! Jeremiah 51:12

We got to our new location about dark and set up camp again. Rex said he hated to do it, but he had to ask us to go on Patrol. He said if he didn't ask us first, the others would say he was playing favorites. We told him, "No problem, Rex. We understand." I took the radio, Harlem the M-60 machine gun, and Bear took his mouth.

We knew he was scared, but he still wanted to be the tough guy. All together, twelve of us were going into the jungle. We had a new Lieutenant who the Captain wanted us to take. We did. We didn't pay much attention to him and could tell he wanted to be or thought he should be in charge. We got to our location that was plotted by Headquarters. The Lieutenant said, "I'm going to recon to the north."

I said, "What?"

"Reconnaissance . . . on our position."

"I know what recon is. We don't do that. We stay in position so we know where everyone is. They shoot mortars and artillery and machine gun fire. We look for enemy movement."

"Look, Sgt., or whatever you are, I'm going to recon to the north. You provide the cover if I need it!"

"Yes, Sir!"

I called Headquarters and told Chris to hold any artillery or mortars until we got him back. He said, "Okay, I don't have any scheduled for an hour."

I remember that night extremely well because you could see fairly well. It was about a half-moon. The Lieutenant had been gone for a while. We heard someone moving to our south. They would take a few steps and then duck down. We couldn't tell how many of them there were. I clicked my M-16 as Harlem chambered his M-60. I don't know why we didn't shoot. We just weren't sure. Harlem and I were the only ones to see him. He came right up on us, and I know he didn't see us. I finally realized it was him (the Lieutenant), and he had a .45 pistol. I pointed my M-16 at him and said, "Sir, you almost died. I don't know why you didn't. Stay here, and don't leave again."

He had gotten lost and couldn't find us. I asked Harlem why he didn't shoot, and he said he didn't know. The rest of the night went well, except I wondered all night what would have happened if I would have shot the Lieutenant. Somebody moved to keep us from pulling that trigger.

We moved back to our location, and they were preparing to move again, further north. It was too quiet where we were . . . couldn't have that! We moved for about six hours into a large dry field that had been sprayed with agent orange. I asked why they sprayed a field, and they told me it was overspray. It was an easy set up, and no patrols went out. There was a village that we could see about a quarter of a mile from us. There were a lot of bomb craters in between where we were and the village. They were full of water. We stayed there a couple of days. It was quiet. We were mortared some at night, but nothing hot. I had gotten to know almost everyone at least by sight, if not by name. I knew very few names. A guy from Baltimore had visited with me a lot. Mostly I wanted to know about Baltimore. I was trying to explain to him that not everyone from Oklahoma was Indian.

There was a guy in Howitzer Battery cutting hair with those old squeeze-type clippers. He had cut our hair.

As we were walking and talking, he saw something on the ground. It looked like a socket. He was a mechanic so he reached down to examine it. It wouldn't budge. I took a few more steps thinking he was through. He kicked it to loosen it, and it blew up. It was an old buried mine. His leg blew to pieces. It went all over me. His other leg was full of shrapnel. He yelled and would not be still, so I couldn't stop the blood flow. About that time, someone grabbed me and threw me to the ground. It was Harlem. I said, "I'm all right."

"Shut up! You are bleeding bad!" I told him it was Baltimore's leg, and that I was okay. They wouldn't believe me and cut my fatigue legs to make sure. They called in a chopper to take him to Bien Hoa Air Base. I never knew for six months what happened to him. He wrote a letter to us after he got home saying the VA was fitting him with a leg. He told us about how much protest was going on in the States. He said Chicago was bad. Men in the United States were getting scared and running to Canada to get out of the draft. Some were even going to prison to keep from serving their country. I wasn't writing home about the truth of this war, and I guess they hadn't told me everything either. We had no choice but to continue to do what we felt we needed to as soldiers.

The brass didn't seem to be happy with us not seeing much contact, so our next move would be going closer to the Cambodian border (not the area we were in before). We went west through thick jungle, rougher terrain. Everything was harder. The bamboos were as tall as elephant grass, 10 to 12 feet tall. We could not see anything. They called in agent orange to be sprayed. It was an herbicide used in undiluted form to kill the foliage. It drifted all over us, but they said it wouldn't hurt us. (Right!) It just kills the foliage in 12 hours. It stuck to you like oil on your skin. We stayed where we were that night, then moved into the sprayed area the next morning. As the sun got hotter, the foliage turned browner and began falling off. We saw bunkers and found some tunnels. Two VC ran out of the bunkers, and the tank with the flamethrower just burned them alive. The diesel stunk, and the flames would shoot 30 to 50 feet. No one even tried to shoot them. We just watched them burn. Bear finally saw something that he couldn't overcome. He said, "That's sickening! What's wrong with you guys? Have you become that hard? Shoot the 'gooks,' but don't burn them alive!"

His questions were one a *normal* person would ask, but it was one I didn't want to face and wasn't going to face. I knew if I admitted he was right, I couldn't go on as I needed to. The foliage was getting brown and the flame-thrower had caught the tall grass on fire, burning 30 feet high. It burned until it hit the area not sprayed.

Bear changed that day. He looked at us differently. He knew something had made us change into people he didn't know or could even like that much. He quit bragging. He realized he was being measured by us for what he did as a soldier, not what he said he could do. Harlem still didn't like him much. I told him, "Don't worry about Bear. He's okay. Even if he did grow up being prejudice, he won't show it around someone as big as you are."

We didn't find much of anything in the bunkers. We set up a tent, used our cots, and stayed in the burned area. There were rats everywhere. They looked as big as cats. I guess the fire had moved them out. We could hear them moving around that night, but could not see them. We just hoped that's what we heard.

The next day we loaded up to move more to the west. We drew occasional sniper fire. Someone told me Chris had been hit by sniper fire while loading his track. The bullet had made a part in his hair and just grazed the top of his head. It didn't bring much blood. He said, "I looked down just as it hit me."

I told him if he hadn't looked down it would have hit him right in the forehead. I remember hearing Chris tell the Captain and his reply was, "Huh, you should have had your helmet on!" We almost always wore our jungle hats. They were light and protected us from the sun, but on a move, we were supposed to wear our steel pots and flak jackets. We made the move and got deeper in the jungle; we went through some small villages and saw some Montagnard Indians. They looked like African people. They were different, even spoke a different language than the South Vietnamese. I didn't think you could be any more primitive than Vietnamese people, but I think they were. However, they were also cleaner. No one bothered them.

As we went on further into the jungle, it looked worse and worse. We started getting the feelings again. We broke through on an old road that went beside a French villa and rubber plantations. There were a few Vietnamese working, but they didn't look at us, just glanced once in a while. We knew that wasn't right. We moved about another five miles before trying to find an area big enough to set up. We had to use a tank with a dozer blade to clear the area; snakes and rats went everywhere. There were spiders that could paralyze you if they bit you, large black ants, and monkeys making eerie noises.

Just one more place to wonder about. I knew I had become hardened to everything. I also knew I had nine and a half more miserable months, but I knew I'd never get out of that place alive. There were too many ways—too many chances for me to die. I was so miserable; I didn't care. I didn't want to be there nine and a half more months! I realized what was happening to me when I didn't care if we burned someone alive. I also knew it was a memory I would always have. If I did get home, how in the world was I going to be any kind of man? How was I going to be a good husband or someday a good father? How could I possibly expect the one I loved to wait for me, marry me, and expect me to be the same man I was when I left? I wasn't handling my life very well. I questioned God. I didn't care if I got back or not. I just did whatever they told me to do. I ended up hurting more people, breaking their hearts. I was trying not to feel sorry for myself, but I just knew my days on earth were surely numbered.

We got camp set up, and I knew there would be a patrol, but I also knew it wasn't our turn. We set up our claymore mines around our perimeter. I put my cot up, careful to keep the bedding off the ground so the rats wouldn't get on it. We shot a few fire missions. We could hear the monkeys around the perimeter. Bear had his cot a couple of feet from mine. He asked about the area we were in. I said, "It doesn't feel good, but I don't think it is as bad as the Iron Triangle we were in before Tet."

I asked him why he was in the Army. He told me he wanted to be a part of this and stand up for our Country. He continued, "Guys are doing everything they can to get out of being here, going to Canada, doing whatever." I told him my story, and we went to sleep.

It seemed like morning came quickly. Rex came over, saying a patrol was going out in a few minutes. He told me he needed a map reader and radio operator. I went to Chris and plotted our exact location and let him know about where we were going. We got our frequency worked out, etc. I went by the FDC tent to say hello to Mike. I hadn't seen him in a while. He was still on a strict shift, but I just said hello to him. I went back, and Rex had gotten 12 men together for the patrol. Harlem was the M-60 machine gunner, and Bear also had an M-60. He looked like Rambo. I said, "We don't take two M-60s on patrol."

"We do today." Rex was going with us. He told me a new 2nd Lieutenant was also going with us.

I said, "That's just great!"

"You'll like him. D Troop is also sending a patrol. It will be about 45 minutes before we leave." I took time to write some letters. As we left, Rex said, "I don't want to pick a point man. Someone want to volunteer?"

Bear replied, "I will."

"You've got the M-60 machine gun. You can't be point." A guy named Gus, from Kentucky, who I didn't know very well, took point. He had been there since January, just before Tet. He had scars all over his face from a car wreck. His dad had retired from the Army so he knew about the Army way. We walked about 100 yards when rocks began to hit us, and they hit hard! We looked around, and the monkeys were throwing rocks at us. Someone was hit with manure. We knew we were not supposed to shoot them, but they were a nuisance. The Lieutenant started laughing and said, "This is something. Come over here and get hit in the face with monkey dung!" We shot a few of them, and the rest scattered.

We came upon a large rubber plantation. It looked like 200 trees lined up—like an orchard would be. The trees were about 18 inches around. We were not supposed to be in there. It didn't show it on the map. We were gathered up too close, trying to figure out what to do, when the VC opened fire on us with AK47s. As I tried to dive on the ground, my radio antenna was extended and the small metal ball on the end of the antenna got hung in the fork of a tree. It made me swing about two feet above the ground. I could see bark flying off the trees and could hear that guys were being hit. It seemed like I was stuck there forever, knowing any minute I would be hit. I couldn't jerk the limb down, so I got out of the radio harness and left it swinging. It was hit, so now we had no radio communication. We probably couldn't call in artillery anyway amidst the rubber trees.

Harlem and Bear were running the M-60s as fast as they could shoot. Our medic was working on a couple of guys. It didn't look like they were real bad. We finally got them off of us and started to do a Search and Destroy Mission. I was still pretty shook up from hanging in the tree. Gus came over to me, saying there wasn't anything he could do to help me. He said, "I can't believe you didn't get hit! Were you praying?"

I said, "Nope, people back home are doing that!"

"They must be doing a good job!" We laughed and went on looking around. What we found didn't look good. The dead VC was part of the North Vietnamese regular army, the kind we saw in Bien Hoa and Saigon. We found four dead—found no bunkers or tunnels. The rubber trees were pretty shot up. We figured our government would be paying for that. We had to evacuate two guys and had to carry them a mile to find a place to pop smoke (get a chopper to land).

We got them loaded without drawing any more fire and got back to our camp a little before dark. We were told we would maintain our position for a few days. We got our mail delivered by chopper with ammunition and nonpotable water. It wasn't full so we had to conserve water. The Mess Tent set up and fed us a hot meal. All my life I had been a picky eater, but it didn't matter now. I even ate boiled cabbage. The mail clerk said we had a new 1st Sergeant, and he would be coming to the field. They told us he had been in a basic training unit in Alabama. This was his first tour in Vietnam. He came the next day. *Was he ever spit shined! He had on his bright yellow Sergeant stripes, name, and U.S. Army all shining, along with his boots. He started inspecting the Mess Tent, First Aid tent, and any place he could inspect. He was telling us to clean our weapons, shave, and put on our steel pots.*

Our Captain was a good guy, but he was getting short. We asked Rex to talk to him. "Don't leave us with this guy!"

Rex said, "It will work out."

That evening the First Sergeant lined us all up and told us we would be moving the next morning. He said, "I want the place cleaned up; leave no paper or cigarette butts. Make sure all your mail is burned. This is the sloppiest bunch I have ever seen."

We looked at Rex. Again, he smiled.

We're in the middle of the jungle. We may leave body parts here, and this guy wants us to pick up our cigarette butts! I'm not going to do it!

Rex was still smiling. "You didn't see what he did to the mechanics today over their tools. Things will work out."

That night, not too long after dark, almost everyone was

still walking around talking. The First Sergeant was in his tent when all of a sudden yellow smoke started coming out from under it. I heard him yell something, and then a concussion grenade went off inside the tent. He came running out in his underwear. It reminded me of Sgt. Taylor.

The next morning a chopper came in, blowing dust everywhere, and picked up the First Sergeant. He didn't even try to find out who put the grenade in his tent. He said nothing to anyone. Rex said, "I told you things would work out. He'll never give anyone a hard time again, even at Base Camp!" In fact, in just a few days, he was transferred, and we never saw him again.

We moved a little closer to Cambodia. We were just on the edge of the Iron Triangle, not nearly as deep as we were before, but it seemed like the jungle just kept getting thicker and thicker. It was so humid; it was difficult to breathe. A few of the guys had asthma, and it was really hard for them, but I was still able to suck on my cigarettes. We got to our new area and began setting up. The Captain told everyone to dig in because we would be here for a while. We dug in and filled our sand bags. It was still dry season, so we didn't worry about them filling up with water. It was a little cooler in them. Mine was never any bigger than to lie down in, and sometimes it was nice to do that and sleep if I could. Some days I could sleep with an 155 Howitzer Fire Mission going on.

Rex came over and said they were going to have to send out patrols that night, but we wouldn't have to go; we would do perimeter watch. I had been there long enough and had seen enough that I knew drugs were what some of the guys were doing to numb their feelings. They locked themselves in their tanks or APC and put themselves in another world far away from where we were. That's how they could relax and cope with the war. I usually knew who they were as did everyone else, but no one cared as long as they were ready when needed. That's all that mattered, and they always were. I had changed so much in four months that I didn't even know myself. There was no need for drugs. It's hard to justify moral upbringing as a reason not to use drugs when I had done and seen so much; drugs seemed minor.

Gus came over and asked if we were going on patrol. I said, "No, Rex told us it would be C Troop." Gus and I had talked several times since he had volunteered to be point man on patrol. He was a good guy. The scars on his face made him look mean. We talked about R & R (Rest and Relaxation). Seven days of leaving this country behind. I wanted to go to Sydney, Australia. The married men wanted Hawaii, so they could meet their wives there. There were lots of places, but I just wanted Sydney. We both applied to go.

After the patrols went out and we were doing perimeter watch, we began getting mortared heavily, and receiving machine gun fire. The patrols were shooting. It was a mess. I heard a mortar coming in on top of us. I couldn't see it, just heard it. Our Captain's tent was just a few feet from where I was. I listened as it hit the ground. It sounded real close, but it didn't explode. We were up all night. The radio contact with the patrols had stopped, no one shooting from their locations. We knew it was bad. It seemed like forever before the sun came up. I knew we were going to go get them. I looked around, and the mortar I had heard was stuck in the ground about 12 feet from where I was and about 5 feet from where our Captain was. I kept thinking about all these close calls and wondering when it was going to catch up with me. At that time, I didn't care. I didn't think God was where I was. I was sure He wasn't there, but someone was moving in all those close calls.

Rex came over as I figured he would and told us we were going. He said he needed 20 men, (which are more than we had ever taken), four machine gunners, and two radios. Our Captain was getting short and he had seen the mortar round by his tent. He said, "I've got some Lieutenants to go with you, if you want them."

Rex replied, "No, the 2nd Lieutenant will be all right.

He went with us before and did pretty well. In fact, most of us liked him. He was drafted. I don't know how in the world he got through Officer Candidate School."

Our Captain told us he would be flown out in a day or two to Base Camp. "My time is over. Last night was too close." He had a wife and two kids back in Georgia. He wished us luck, as we did him. He was especially close to Rex . . . both being from Georgia. It was unusual for enlisted men to socialize or become friends, but in Vietnam, we did. Harlem asked Rex how long we were going to be out there, and he said he didn't know but hoped it was just today.

"Well, why is the Captain telling us bye now?" Harlem asked Rex.

Rex lowered his head and replied, "This ain't good, be ready to go."

Rex told me to go get the maps from Chris and radio frequencies and to also get air clearance before we went. He said for us to make sure Fire Direction Control was ready. "I'm making you a Sergeant or Specialist 5. Your MOS and what you are doing don't fit, so you will be a Buck Sgt. while you're here. You'll be a platoon leader before long, but for now, you're a tank commander. I'm going to move Joe."

"We lost so many men; we had to spread out just to keep the APCs we have now going." Also, he told Harlem that he'd be an E-4 right away. We were ready to go. We had a new medic. He had loaded himself down with half the medical supplies—too much to try and carry. Rex got him straightened out and told him not to expect to find too many alive. "We lost all radio contact last night—haven't heard from any of them."

We started moving toward the first location. Gus was back with me. I didn't know who was on point. I was kind of glad that I didn't know. The first location was empty. We could find no one and no blood. We went to the second location and found five guys dead that had been *messed with* by the VC. It wasn't the first time I had seen that, but this was so sickening that I lost it again. The new medic was almost in shock. Bear told me, "Now I can see how you can be so full of hate for those people. Now the burning with the flame thrower wouldn't bother me."

I have tried to write as accurately as I can in describing the horrible acts of war. Every combat vet knows of all the cursing and talk that goes on during your entire stay in the Army. However, it is no longer in my heart to talk that way. I want friends and families of Veterans to be able to read this so I haven't filled it with vulgar language. Every combat vet also knows what being *messed with* means. We have all seen it. There's no need for me to explain, except to say that David did more than just hit Goliath with a rock.

We got the bodies in bags and started moving into the third location, hoping we'd find the rest of the guys there. We walked right into their location. They were all alive, almost out of ammo, and a few had minor wounds. Their medic had already taken care of all the patrols. They had moved in together to try and defend themselves. They were under heavy fire and had to leave the dead behind. We didn't tell them right then what had happened to them. Their Lieutenant had told them to turn their radios off because of the noise. He's the same one who we almost shot.

Rex said, "Sir, I think the VC know exactly where we are." He immediately radioed back to tell the Captain of their status.

The Captain said, "All of you come in now. There's heavy VC movement in the area."

Rex asked if we thought we had enough men to carry everyone out and get all the equipment. We started trying to get everything together when we began drawing heavy machine gun fire. We ducked down and could hear the mortars starting to be dropped into the tubes. Rex yelled, "Call in! We need artillery now!"

I called in to Chris and told him our location and the

Howitzers began to fire. The whistling of the big rounds were going over our heads. It was very eerie. The Lieutenant was really mad about me doing it. He said, "You got an E-4 calling in artillery over our heads?"

Rex answered, "Yes, Sir, an E-4 who knows what he is doing!" No one told him most of the coordinates and clearances had been worked out before we left. It didn't take very long for the VC to stop shooting, and we could get ready to leave again.

The Lieutenant said, "I'm going to take a few men and do a body count." Our Lieutenant was a 2nd Lieutenant so he was outranked, but Rex was running the show.

"Sir, you're crazy. You're not taking any of my men anywhere! If you want to get a body count, you go, and we'll bring a body bag for you."

"I'm reporting you to the Captain!"

"Okay, Sir, I'll go with you, *if* we can get out of here."

We got back and gave the commanding officer and Captain a full report. He had made connections and was going to be picked up the next day. He told the Lieutenant that he would not have a chance to get anyone else killed. He said, "You'll be going back to Base Camp with me and be the landing zone officer."

That was a filthy job. The choppers and Chinooks made so much dust that you couldn't breathe or see, and he would have to stay out there all day.

The Executive Officer was in charge after the Captain left. He let Rex run most everything. We stayed there almost two weeks with very little activity. I saw Chris and told him my 30 days without a shower was almost there. My hair was so matted that I couldn't get a comb through it. Chris told me the brass was talking about going back to Base Camp in a couple of days or so. I was ready. Rex said how great it would be to go back to Bien Hoa Air Force Base.

"Yes, it would, but I'll be happy with Base Camp." We finally got to go back. A shower never felt so good—a hot meal, a cot, and a metal roof over my head. Rex had told me I'd probably go back to Headquarters and work with Chris and Ronnie. That sounded great! I wrote letters, cleaned my weapon, did everything that needed to be done, and went to the PX to get restocked on toothpaste, cigarettes, and anything else I needed. I had been paid three or four times, $38.00 a payday, and still had almost all of it. Money just didn't seem too important.

CHAPTER 7
SOUTHERN CROSS

And God said, "This is the sign of the covenant I am making between me and you and every living creature with you, a covenant for all generations to come. I have set my rainbow in the clouds, and it will be the sign of the covenant between me and the earth." Genesis 9: 12–13

Gus and I found out our R&R had not been approved. We'd have to wait 30 more days. We stayed in Base Camp almost 3 weeks. We had a new 1st Sgt. He also decided to stay in Base Camp. Most important of all, we got a new Captain. He looked and acted like a Boy Scout! It was his first combat duty. He wasn't a "respect me" freak, just different. He didn't want anyone to know he didn't know much, but he would still ask questions. He carried a locked, shiny, black leather briefcase and wore air-borne, spit-shined boots. He was bald headed and had a Hitler-type moustache. He was really anxious to get in the field and didn't have to wait long because we were short on officers.

Rex said, "I hope he doesn't take the Lieutenant off the LZ." Apparently, Captain Holt had written something in his report that told our new Captain to leave him where he was. We were happy with our new 2nd Lieutenant who was more like one of us. Working in Headquarters, I heard the intelligence officers and our Lt. Colonel (Squadron Commander) talking about him, questioning whether they should leave him in Headquarters or put someone else in charge of B Troop. I don't think they had anyone else. Our Executive Officer, 1st Lieutenant, was experienced and could handle the job so they did hold him back some.

He joined us in about 30 days. We had gone north again to an area that was more of a rice paddy area, with several villages nearby. We took a platoon of South Vietnamese troops. We very seldom took them with us. We had to watch our things pretty closely, and they just wouldn't fight. They were notorious for getting Americans into trouble. They were heavy into the black market—cigarettes, drugs, and women. They always had a way to get whatever they wanted. I was never comfortable with them. My heart went out to the South Vietnamese children, but at times, I was bitter towards the adults who were supposed to be helping us fight "their" war. Our interpreter was from Hanoi. His family lived there.

Here I was again trying to figure out what was going on. As an average GI, I just knew what I saw and what I felt. I didn't see them doing anything to help themselves. They traded in real young girls, drugs, American beer, and cigarettes. The only time we had beer was when we were at Base Camp. They carried American rifles and wore our boots. I'm not going to dwell on the South Vietnamese Army nor will I say they were all that way. I know some gave their lives for the South. I'm just talking about the ones I saw and was asked to fight with. The Brass thought we would be well served by having them with us as we went into the villages and walked the dikes of the rice paddies.

As we walked into the villages with the ARVNs, I was trying to watch the villagers' eyes as they were questioned about any enemy movement. They never told us the truth. Sometimes the ARVNs were rougher on them than they should have been. They were scared. If the North Vietnamese had been there and they had told us, the North would have killed them and taken everything they had. They were truly the innocent, hard-working people, just trying to stay alive. The kids would hang onto us to give them what we had. We always carried extra C-rations just to give to the children. I had nieces and nephews at home not much older than some of those kids, and I truly was thankful I was an American and none of my family had to live like that.

The orders we had not to shoot into a village even if we were drawing fire made sense to me. A grass hut doesn't stop bullets, and those children lived in those grass huts. You still just couldn't trust anyone, especially when you had the ARVNs with you. The VC would tie bombs to the children, and they would walk right up to you. What a mess! Deep inside me, I was crying out to God—never in a prayerful way, but in a bitter and angry manner. I wanted to know where He was and why this was happening—why we, as GIs or as human beings, were in such a dark, sinful place. I had completely shut God out, except when I was bitter or angry at what was going on. I felt like I had aged twenty years in six months. I shouldn't have to be dealing with all of this.

We walked out in the rice paddies where most of the village was working. They had about six oxen; everything else was done by hand. The paddies of rice and water looked stagnant. It stunk like sewer. In fact, when they needed to go to the bathroom they just squatted down and went, both men and women. The oxen flopped wherever. The Vietnamese believed that when "Uncle Joe" died, he came back as an ox, so they took very good care of their oxen.

We went back to where we were camped, and our Captain had been flown in. He told us we would go on patrol that night in the rice paddy area. I thought about having to smell that all night. We really had not seen much enemy activity in that area. Rex was really getting short. We all liked him and hated to lose him, but naturally, we were glad he had made it and was going home to Georgia in a few days.

The Captain really wanted to go with us, but Rex told him that he was needed more at the camp, not on an ambush patrol. We still thought he was some sort of a Boy Scout, but we were amazed that he listened to Rex and truly wanted his advice and was willing to accept it. We saw so many Sergeants come over with their own agendas, who ended up putting lives in danger. I didn't know how to take a Captain, who was a troop commander, who could have done whatever he wanted to do, yet who listened to a Sergeant and took his advice. It was obvious that Captain Dales really wanted to go and could have gone.

Rex got us ready to go on the night patrol. There wasn't much of a place to get except on the berms of the rice paddies. We still had most of the same group; Bear and Harlem on the machine guns, Gus, Rex, our 2nd Lt., a couple of new guys, and I was operating the radio. There were twelve of us all together. Captain Dales talked to me a lot about our locations, radio frequencies, and call signs. He really seemed okay. He just looked so much like a Boy Scout, but when he asked you a question, he was truly interested in what was going on. He had graduated from a military academy and knew procedure by the book, but he didn't impose that on us. He understood that this was not a conventional war. We all appreciated his openness to us.

We got ready to go into the rice paddies. This was the first time I had been in the middle of rice paddies. I just remembered the smell from earlier in the day. We got there and had some difficulty getting into a good position on the berms. We finally figured it out and were talking some. I know our voices were carrying over the water. We never smoked on Patrol because of the light it projected.

We sat there almost five hours before the machine gun fire started pouring in on us—seemed like from every direction. The red tracers were going over our heads as we went into the water and used the berm for protection. We were not in a good position to even shoot back. Those tracers looked like they were only about six inches over the berm. I had the radio on my back and no way to keep it dry. I couldn't raise myself up enough to get it off my back. The water was about a foot deep, and it felt like there was another foot of silt and mud. I rolled over on my back so I could keep my head up. My M-16 was stuck in the muck. I tried to get it out as I was trying to keep my head out of the water. I had that junk in my face, and it was all I could do to keep my head up. The radio kept sinking me into the silt . . . or whatever it was. I heard no one from the patrol shooting. Harlem was close enough to me that I could talk to him. He had his M-60 in the muck and was trying to get it out without getting his head too high. It turned out to be a terrible place to try and defend ourselves, especially the way we were scattered out. We felt helpless. The machine gun fire seemed to be all over the place. None of us were shooting back so it looked as if they were just shooting and didn't know exactly where we were. We lay there as they shot over our heads, missing us by only a few inches. Rex didn't feel like they were moving any closer to us.

I felt something crawling on me and hoped it wasn't a snake. I couldn't handle that, but Sgt. Rex said they were leaches, and they'd come off later. That was such a creepy feeling. I was lying in a rice paddy that I couldn't stand to smell, with leaches stuck to me, yet it was saving my life. My radio kept sinking and pulling me deeper into the water. I was trying to unhook myself from it without raising up. I finally managed to cut the heavy canvas webbing that held the radio to me so I could get free, making it a little easier, and I could pull some of the leaches off of me.

I lay there looking up, as they kept shooting, and I thought about what it must have been like for the 101st Airborne . . . one of the largest jumps and one of the few where over 100 men jumped landing in rice paddies. Eighty-five percent of them were killed or wounded. Some drowned as the eighty pounds of equipment on their backs pulled them down. It was one of the largest disasters in Vietnam. They had no chance. I was just glad I didn't have to see it . . . 85 percent . . . what a tremendous loss! As far as I knew, all twelve of us were still alive, none of us was shooting back, and we had no communication.

It was a clear night. The monsoon season had begun, but

this night it was clear. I looked up at the tracers going by and saw the Southern Cross in the sky. It had almost a hazy line going from star to star. What a powerful display of God! I felt betrayed by God again—asking Him why we couldn't see it in North America. I couldn't understand why it could be seen in a place as awful as this. I felt like God was way out there, far, far away.

Several years later, I received my answers. I do remember it was a beautiful night and the first time I had ever noticed it while being there. I was sure it was the first time I had cried. I told God if He was ready to take me, then I knew I was ready. I felt like He was giving me more than I could stand. I could not see what He was doing. I just knew how miserable I was. We didn't know what the new Captain could do to help us. The radio was buried, and we weren't sure where everyone was. The only thing we could do was wait.

I asked Harlem if he saw the Southern Cross in the sky. He said, "Yeah, it makes me think of my grandma . . . she's probably praying for me. When I was little, she made sure I got saved. She thinks angels are keeping those bullets above our heads."

I said, "That's exactly what my granny would say. She prays for me every day, probably all day. It doesn't seem like God is here, but we've made it through a lot of stuff for something or somebody not to be helping us. We still have a long time to go. Do you feel in your heart you're going to leave here walking?"

"No, not if we stay in the field."

"Yeah, look where we are right now! I don't know where to shoot, if to shoot, or how anybody is going to help us. Our new Captain Dales doesn't know where we are."

In just a few minutes, we heard the loud diesel engines of the tanks and APCs coming toward us and saw the lights on bright, but they weren't firing. The bullets going over our heads slowed down. The tanks pulled up to the edge of the rice paddies. They began to shoot M-60 and 50-caliber machine guns, probably 10 feet above our heads. The shells stopped coming. We began to crawl toward the APCs. I pulled on my radio trying to get it out, but it wouldn't budge so I left it. Amazingly, all of us got back to our APC, no one hurt, just wet with leaches stuck to us. We rode back to our camp and went into the Headquarters tent where there was light. Captain Dales was standing there with his steel pot and flak jacket on. He was one of the ones on the APC who came and got us. He explained to us that he didn't really know what to do. He asked me about the radio. I told him.

He cautioned, "Son, you should've drowned with it, especially if you didn't shoot it or disable it. The enemy can receive our transmissions."

"Yes, Sir!"

He continued, "In the morning, you can go get it." We left after that and went back to our APCs to dry off and change our clothes. The leaches had made bright red spots on us, and we smelled like a sewer.

Rex came up to me saying the new Captain had really done the only thing he could do to help us. "What he said about the radio is bull. I'll talk to him in the morning. Don't worry about it! I'm about ready to get out of this place, maybe day after tomorrow. I got pretty shook up tonight. You get scared when your time gets close. Did you see the Southern Cross tonight?"

I said, "Yeah, I guess we all did."

"You think that's why we got out of there tonight?"

"Well, something happened," I told him.

We dried off and changed clothes. The medic brought some salve for us to use where the leaches had been. It kind of deadened the sting.

The next morning the Captain came looking for me. He said, "Last night was my first combat experience. I've been to all the war colleges, but actually being here is much different. I expected to receive radio contact and coordinates. When

I received none, I didn't know how to react. Sgt., I realize you are an experienced trooper and a good one. I don't need any of you to drown, so forget what I said last night. I was pretty shook up."

"Thank you, Sir, and thank you for saving us last night. I don't know if we would've gotten out of there without your doing what you did."

He shook my hand and said, "Let's start over!"

"Okay, Sir."

I asked him if we were moving today, and he told me he didn't know yet. We got word later in the day that we were staying put. An engineer group was pinned down and needed our artillery support. The Big Red One had been choppered in for support, but had no artillery support. The Howitzer Battery was getting ready to use all their guns, not the usual two or three for backup. They were running everywhere, getting shells and powder ready for a large fire mission. Harlem was recruited to carry ammunition. It was heavy and he was really strong. Bear and I were on perimeter watch, kind of kicked back on the M-60 machine guns, talking and smoking. We opened a new case of C-rations and discussed how unusual it was to have all the artillery ready and none of our guys in trouble. We knew some of the Howitzer guys. They worked hard. Those shells were heavy and hard to handle. Gun bunny was the name they were stuck with.

We started hearing on the radio that the Engineers needed support, but we were having trouble getting air clearance. Some Lt. Colonel was flying around looking. Until he came down, they could not get air clearance. Finally, we began shooting all guns at a rapid rate. I wondered how many troops had been killed while the Lt. Colonel was looking around in the air. Sometimes it seemed to me that at the top level of brass there was some disorganization. When something went wrong, some of the Captains and Majors got the blame. I guess that was the way it worked everywhere, but there were some good brave officers that were relieved of their command because of a blunder made by someone higher up. Most were career soldiers, and once relieved of their command, their careers were over. It was really unfair, but what was fair? (Enough of that.)

The Howitzer firing was so rapid the noise was tremendous. They were loading at an unbelievable rate. Bear and I saw a ball of fire come out the hatch of a 155 Howitzer. At first, I thought it was hit by a mortar, but the fire was blue and yellow; a mortar was bright orange. We soon realized the inside of the Howitzer was on fire with three men inside it, burning up. A Sgt. came out of the small door hatch. He hit his head on the metal above it cutting his forehead wide open, blood spewing everywhere. Bear was in front of me as we were running toward the Howitzer. We were about 20 feet from it when someone yelled, "The ammo will blow! Everyone move back!" I hesitated for a few seconds, but Bear didn't change his pace, he just kept running. Someone handed me a fire extinguisher. One of the crew came out of the door burning from his boots to his head. I sprayed him until the fire was out, and the medic took over. Bear went in and got the other guy out. It was too late for him. His lungs were burned up. Several of the other guys brought fire extinguishers to put the fire out and stabilize the powder and ammo inside the Howitzer. Those guys were shooting so fast, trying to help save their lives on the other end. All the other guns were still firing. The tube of the barrel was supposed to be swabbed or cooled off between each round, but for speed's sake, they weren't doing that. The powder came in cloth bags in a pellet form. When the powder was placed in the tube, the heat caused it to catch fire. I didn't know the other two guys but was acquainted with the Sergeant. We knew his wife had left him, and he was having a difficult time dealing with it. That happened to a lot of guys. There was nothing they could do about it. We got all of them medevacked out.

Bear and I went back to our APC. Harlem was there waiting for us. "I saw what you guys did. You're crazy; you must think your granny has a direct line to God. Everyone else stopped, but you two just kept going!"

I said, "I hesitated a moment, did some soul searching, but Bear kept going. If he would have stopped, I may have, too. I don't know; it's just something you do when it's your turn. Those guys were burned so badly. I don't know if they will make it. We'll probably never know."

I'm always feeling sorry for myself. Those guys' lives are ruined; one is dead. I think about the memory embedded in my mind of more burning bodies and the way it smelled. There is so much already to shut out. How will we do it? Harlem spoke softly, "There is a reason we saw that cross last night."

"I guess, seems to be a reason for everything in this place. The rainy season is starting, and it will last for six months. All the dust turns to mud."

Bear said, "Yeah, they get about eight feet of rain in six months."

"That's what they say. I can't imagine all this dust becoming mud. I'm sick of breathing this dirt."

We shot fire missions most of the night and some after the sun rose and were really tired. We heard the engineers had gotten it pretty bad but never really knew for sure. We never did know what they were doing. They got the Big Red One out of there and brought in B52s, carpet-bombing. Those things shook the ground. We could feel it inside our APC. We had seen B52s before but were never quite this close, and we always went into the area afterwards. This time we didn't. We knew we were moving the next day.

CHAPTER 8

R & R

Six days you shall labor, but on the seventh day you shall rest; even during the plowing season and harvest you must rest. Exodus 34:21

———————————————

Gus came over and said the Captain wanted to talk to us. "I hope it's our R&R. I'm ready!"

The Captain told us we had been turned down again for R&R in Sydney. He felt bad and told us if we would go to Bangkok, Thailand, he could get us there for sure next month. "I'll have three openings."

"I'm ready," I replied.

"Me too!" Gus chimed.

So at least we knew that in thirty days, if we made it, we were getting out of there for seven days. Gus knew a guy from Howitzer Battery who had been there so we talked to him about it. We were excited about going, getting to clean up, and wearing civilian clothes. I was still writing home on a regular basis, and I asked my family to send me $300.00 from the money I had been sending home. I told them to wait two weeks, and then send the money orders to me.

We moved the next day, and it went real well. The Captain was doing well, and everyone was getting used to him. We had very little contact. Rex had flown out and was on his way home.

He was a good Sergeant and would stand up for his men. I was so glad he made it.

I got my first in country letter. I couldn't believe it. It was from my cousin who had been drafted and was fighting north of me. He was in the jungle and had been for a while. He wrote the real stuff to me. I wrote back to him trying to raise his spirits. As bad as I felt like I had it, there were lots of guys walking over twenty miles every day, if they made it. My cousin made it out, but he became addicted to drugs and alcohol and spent a lot of time in mental institutions. It ruined his life.

We didn't have much activity going on. We had gotten rid of the ARVNs from South Vietnam. I was resting easier with them gone. I knew we were supposed to be working with them. It was their Country, but they weren't like Bear, Rex, Gus, or Harlem who would fight with you and for you. There were thousands of Americans that laid down their lives for the South Vietnamese people, so to see them run and let us die for their Country didn't fit into any of my beliefs. They weren't all like that, I know.

It was going to take a long time to win this war, moving from place to place, along with the restrictions we had on us. I tried not to think of the politics and all that was going on in the world. I knew there was nothing I could do except fight with the guys I trusted, until my time was up—one way or the other. I was still anxious about my R&R, hoping I would make it.

We went to a new area and set up. It was pretty wooded for us to set up in, but the dozer had made an LZ, making the area sandy and dirty, but our Lt. Colonel could land his chopper.

They flew in some water to drink and also some non-potable water for showers. We had heard we were going to get a new full Colonel. We heard that George Patton III wanted to be in command of the only fully armored cavalry regiment in Vietnam. We also heard he had extended his stay in 'Nam just to get us. We didn't know what to expect, but as I mentioned earlier, there were some problems at the top, and we knew something needed to be done.

The mess tent was cooking fried chicken, mashed potatoes, and gravy. We were having white bread and milk . . . unbelievable! It smelled so good. Captain Dales said he got it done for us. I didn't know if he really did or not, but we were so happy. I said, "We didn't get fried chicken, even at the Air Force Base." I had just gotten my plate and sat down when a chopper came in to the LZ, dirt flew everywhere—all over the food. I covered it up with my arms as best I could. It still got dirt on it, but I ate it anyway. We all did, and it was so good.

We saw a big man get out of the chopper with a white German shepherd. He had some pearl handled .45s. He went straight into the Headquarters Tent. He was the man, George Patton III. Chris came over where we were saying, "He may be all right . . . at least he talked to us." Chris was getting close to going home. Ronnie had a new guy training him. I thought I might move over there. Chris said he thought I might, also, but he continued, "Our new Captain Dales likes you and doesn't want to move you, except when we are in Base Camp."

"Yeah, when is that going to be?"

"No one knows. Maybe Colonel Patton will get us more organized. We may hook up with 2nd Squadron and sweep a large area north of here." I told Chris that Gus and I were going on R&R in 26 more days.

"Where are you going?"

"Bangkok, Thailand. I gave up on Sydney, Australia."

"You'll have a good time, just to get out of here is enough." We stayed there another couple days. We may have lost a couple of guys on Patrol from D Troop, but I didn't have to go. We did join up with 2nd Squadron to make the large sweep. Colonel Patton was always observing from his chopper. As we were going through the jungle, he gave us directions. He also called in another B52 carpet bombing. A few jets came in first and dropped some white phosphorous. Sometimes, some older prop planes came in to drop bombs. They looked so slow and had to come in so low. I thought they might be hit by their own bombs. They looked like sitting ducks. We never saw any of them shot down, but we knew there had been lots of pilots lost and detained in POW camps in North Vietnam.

After the bombing stopped, we went in to sweep the area. The craters from the bombs were huge; some were 15 feet deep or deeper. The white phosphorous was still burning. If anyone was killed, we didn't find any part of them. We started drawing fire and could not see anything but jungle. We shot back. The Colonel got on the radio saying, "You are shooting at C Troop, and C Troop is shooting at B Troop." We couldn't see. We stopped, and they stopped the shooting. No one got hurt.

We swept the area for several days but found very little. Someone kept ordering agent orange to be sprayed all around us. It drifted on us. It was everywhere. We laid in it, slept in it, ate it, and drank it, but we knew it was just killing trees. (That's what they told us.) The constant rain was more depressing than the heat. Every time I thought it couldn't get worse, it did. The jungle was unbearable. It was so humid that you couldn't breathe. Steam came off our heads. The red dirt seeped from the pores of our skin. I had never had a steam bath and wondered if that is what it felt like. I was used to staying wet with sweat, but now I was staying wet with rain. It would flood six to eight inches every day in the flat lands.

Harlem said one good thing about the wet weather was we couldn't smoke as much because we couldn't keep our cigarettes dry. "It's not as hazardous to our health." You had to really look hard to find humor in anything but that made me laugh.

Sometimes you could feel the lightning tingle as it hit trees or water or whatever it hit. It seemed like there were lightning storms every night. I really felt good carrying a radio with a ten-foot antenna stuck in the air. Bear said, "I wonder how many guys get hit with lightning in this war."

"There are probably some, but if I'm one, don't let them

tell my Mama. I didn't come ten thousand miles to get hit by lightning," I told him.

"God ain't going to take us out. Some idiot or the enemy might, but God ain't." Gus and I were getting close to leaving for R&R. My money from home hadn't come yet. The Captain sent us back to Base Camp. I checked the mail before I left. It was still not there at Base Camp. There were two bags of mail at the LZ ready to load on the chopper. I told the Lieutenant I needed to look in them to see if my mail was in there. If it wasn't, I couldn't go on R&R.

"How long you been here?"

"Seven months, Sir."

"I'll send a Private to watch you as you look through it. I shouldn't do this." I'm sure if he had remembered me, he would not have. He was the same Lieutenant that Captain Holt had sent there.

Anyway, it was there . . . three one hundred dollar money orders and some very large civilian clothes. I had lost about 25 lbs. in the field. I went to the PX and got some shirts and pants. Gus and I were ready. The third person going with us was the guy in Howitzer Battery who had been there before. This would be his second R&R. "I didn't know you could do that," I said to him.

"No one else put in for it so I took it."

Gus said, "Good, he knows his way around."

We cleaned up and rode a mud-slinging jeep to Bien Hoa. It felt so weird not to have my M-16. It had grown to me, and I hadn't gone anywhere without it. I couldn't help but think of the guys in the jungle and wishing they could feel the way I was feeling right then. The streets were still a mess from Tet, and some of the smell seemed to be lingering in the air. Kids' bikes and Vietnamese people were everywhere. We drove to the pavilion where we had been in December. The view hadn't changed—troops going home, troops coming in, and body bags on the runway. We got on a military plane of some sort and flew to Bangkok, Thailand—seemed like a couple of hours. We exited the plane, went to a large building for orientation to the country, heard all the rules—what we could and could not do, when to get back, and how serious it was not to come back.

Larry, the guy with Gus and me, told the bus driver which hotel we wanted to stay in . . . the one with maid and laundry service. The complete 5-night package was $55.00 a week, $11.00 a night. A cab driver was outside on call and would take us anywhere we wanted to go for the week for $20.00 apiece. He spoke good English.

They had a different language than the Vietnamese did, but it all sounded the same to me. It really got on my nerves. It was just something else I had to shut out. We saw about everything in Bangkok, had a great five days, drank and smoked a lot, and felt free. When our time was over, I had $10.00 left in Thai money. I gave it to the cab driver. The bus came to get us. The sickest feeling I ever had came over me. I wanted to run. I did not want to get on that bus. It was the hardest step I ever took. This time I knew exactly where I was going, what I would see, and the things I would have to do. It was a sick, nauseating feeling. I knew I had to go back so I went to the airport. We didn't talk much; we just rode the plane back to Bien Hoa. Larry commented, "I've had that feeling twice now. It's hard to come back."

I said, "I don't want to leave again until and if I go home."

I had made a voice recording to send home, and all my family sent one back to me. It was great to hear everyone. My sister told me she was getting married, but was going to wait until I got home to have a January wedding. I still had five months to go, and I didn't want her to do that. I wanted her to go ahead with her life. I knew no one in my family really knew what a mess I was in, except maybe my dad who wrote me once saying he appreciated the letters I was writing, but he knew there was more I was going through. He thanked me for not sharing it with my mother.

I had completely messed up my own relationship with my fiancée, because I was so sure I was not coming home. I didn't want her waiting for me, because even if I got back, I was afraid I couldn't handle the world. Her father was also a WWII veteran. He had told her how war changes people. He had seen it and had seen men come back not fit for society, which had helped her to have some understanding of what was happening to me. I did some things wrong; my judgment was very bad. I really wanted my sister to get married and to leave me out of it. I had another 150 days of that hell to deal with.

We landed at Bien Hoa Air Base. We were picked up by the Supply Sergeant, and we went back to Base Camp. It was raining when we got back. It was wet and muddy. The Sergeant told us to change clothes, and he'd take us to the LZ because they needed us back out in the field.

"Welcome back, guys! You think we could go by the PX for some cigarettes and stuff?" I asked him.

"Okay, we can do that," he told us. Gus had also made Sgt. E-5. Larry was still an E-4. He was older and bigger than both of us. He was going to be out of the Army as soon as he left Vietnam (in about three months). I had five months left, and Gus had six months. The Supply Sgt. took us back to the LZ, and it was raining and storming hard. We were soaked again, waiting on a chopper. The Sgt. left us there.

The Lieutenant at the LZ said, "We can't get a chopper in or out so come back in the morning." We walked back to our hooch and told the Supply Sergeant what happened and thanked him for letting us walk the mile and a half in the rain and mud. We dried off and lay down on our cots. The 1st Sgt. walked in and told us Colonel Patton had ordered everyone with 30 days or less back to a rear area to do mail or whatever, but he wanted them out of the field. That was great news. I was tired of seeing guys with a few days left getting killed.

111

We said, "Maybe this guy is human!" That was one of the best moves that had been made as far as we were concerned.

CHAPTER 9
MY CAPTAIN DALES

This is how we know what love is: Jesus Christ laid down his life for us. And we ought to lay down our lives for our brothers. 1 John 3:16

We went to sleep early and got up ready to go. We ate at the Mess Hall and went back to the LZ. We flew out on a Chinook, taking supplies to our unit. They had moved once since we left and set up in more of an open field, but it was not a rice paddy area. It just flooded six inches deep when it rained. We had a new E-6 Sgt. that had replaced Rex. Gus and I met him before unloading our equipment, but he was scared to death. I think I could have said, *"BOO!"* and he would have run off. Gus said, "Ain't we lucky?"

"This is the fourth sergeant I've had. Maybe this one is too scared to mess with us. I'll go find Harlem and Bear and see what they say." They laughed when I asked them about him.

Bear said, "His name is Hines. We call him Hines 57. He is scared to death of everything and especially Harlem!"

"Everybody is scared of Harlem. He's a big ugly booger from New York City." We continued to talk about my R&R. Harlem was going in 30 days to Singapore. He was sending his money home as most of us were. I told him not to wait as long as I did for his family to send his money for R&R.

We stayed in that location longer than anywhere I had

been. There wasn't much activity. Sgt. Hines had us go on patrol a few times but never went with us. He always had something to do. He didn't know how to call in artillery. He was glad for me to do it. I didn't mind that, but I didn't want to be in charge, having to tell guys where to go and what to do. Gus and I always talked it over and asked for volunteers. If we didn't get one, we would do it. Neither of us wanted that responsibility when lives were on the line. We were thankful that we had good guys who knew the spot we were in and took the burden off of us.

Captain Dales told Gus and me to get a patrol together, a good group. He told us we were coordinating now to join up with another patrol west of here, next to Cambodia. I said, "Isn't that Sergeant Hines's job?"

"Yes, it is, but I asked you to do it."

"Yes, Sir."

"This is important. Sergeant Hines is not going, so you get good guys."

"I can do that."

Gus and I were really disgusted. We both automatically thought it was the South Vietnamese Army we would be joining up with. We wanted good men, but felt we may be losing our best men. Gus said, "Let's go talk to him."

"Okay, if it's South Vietnamese, Sgt. Hines can go and get his own men!"

Captain Dales completely understood our position and said, "Have you not learned to trust me a little? Have I not earned a little respect?"

I answered, "Yes, Sir, you have, and that's why we feel free to tell you our situation with the men."

"Okay, listen, I would never send you to meet the South Vietnamese Army. You are meeting with ten guys from New Zealand."

"I didn't know they were over here."

"There are a few, and they are good so get your guys together."

"Yes, Sir!"

Gus said, "I will never question anything he does again. He ain't no Boy Scout. He's a good soldier and leader."

"I agree."

Chris had left for home, and the new guy they had trained was in Headquarters. He was another guy from Texas. I told him, "You got my job. I was supposed to be in here, and you get an APC."

He said, "Sgt., I'm just doing what they told me to do."

"I know; we all are. I'm just kidding you. Just don't call artillery in on top of me." He had already plotted our meeting place on the map and was aware of what was going on.

He wanted to know if I operated the radio, and I told him I would. "Why?"

"I can't understand those guys; it's a different kind of English."

"Okay, I'll take care of the radio. What's your name, anyway?"

"Shelly."

"Shelly? I'm not calling you that. We're in Vietnam. What's your last name?"

"It's Shelly. My first name is Jacob."

"Okay, Jacob. That's good. You join the Army?"

"Yes, I did. I wanted to fight for my Country, and I wanted to learn a trade."

"I'm not sure where you can use it, but you'll learn a trade!" It seemed strange to me that guys were looking at me with respect and wanted my opinion. I didn't feel worthy. I know I had learned some things, mostly I figured it was because of what I'd done and seen. I was a Sgt. E-5 and so was Gus. We carried a large load. Our leader by rank, Sgt. Hines, was so nervous he was scary to be around, so the Captain put us in charge.

We left the next morning to meet with the New Zealand troop, about 3.5 miles away. They were exactly where they were supposed to be. Two of them were officers. They were all big guys, 6'3" or 6'4," clean, neat, and well equipped. They had been choppered in. We greeted each other. They were New Zealand Special Forces, professional all the way. We were dirty, sloppy, and looked like a rag tag bunch. He asked, "You got combat experience?"

"Yes, we do have, but I don't even know what our mission is!"

"We find 'gooks' and kill 'em. We need some tunnel rats."

"We have some guys that will go into tunnels, but we don't have a K-9 tunnel rat troop." I looked pretty small to him.

He asked, "You a rat?" Being 6' tall and weighing only 145 pounds, I guess he thought I was.

"Sir, I'm not going in a tunnel. I did once, and I ain't going back, but we have guys that will."

We were going on a night sweep. We had never done that before. We didn't tell him that. I radioed back to the Captain and talked to Jacob about what we were doing and the direction we were heading. The New Zealanders couldn't wait until dark. Gus asked, "Are these guys as mean as they look?" I sure hoped so.

I didn't know there was an enemy complex of bunkers about one mile west of us. The New Zealanders knew where it was and couldn't wait to get there. The officer told us all that there would be bamboo spear pits and trip wires, so we were to follow them. We crawled for the mile, and the New Zealand guys found an opening as soon as we got there. They told us the tunnels were active (underground tunnels used by the enemy to hide from us) so to be careful and be quiet. A small ray of light was coming from the opening, meaning the tunnel was occupied.

We had a little guy with us who always volunteered for that stuff. This was different. It was night, and we knew for sure it was occupied. I wasn't sure he would go, and I wasn't going to make him. If I wasn't going, I wasn't going to make anyone else go, but 'Little Tim' said, "I'll go."

The NZ troops were working quietly, enlarging the opening. They were already entering the tunnel. They took knives and machetes. About five or six of them went in. I asked, "What are we supposed to do, just wait?"

"If they don't show up before long, we'll go in with the M-60 machine gunners." I looked at Harlem and could see his eyes and teeth shining in the dark.

"Sgt., I hope they come out!"

"So do I!"

We waited for what seemed like forever when a couple of them finally came out. "There weren't but six 'gooks' down there. Monte got 12 ears." That was a signature of a tunnel rat— ear collection. The other four came out within thirty minutes. They were disappointed.

"There's lots of ammunition and weapons. You know how to get artillery in here?"

"Yes, Sir!"

"Use a fuse delay."

"I know that, and I also know we need to get back! Yeah, and it's probably safe to walk in a single file." We did that, and I called in artillery in about a 500 yd. x 500 yd. area. I told them to use fuse delay—let the shell hit and penetrate the ground before exploding. If a shell hit over a tunnel, it would go into it before exploding. If we thought there was a lot of enemy on the ground, we used a time fuse that exploded before it hit the ground. The artillery came in for three hours. It had blown up everything. There were large caches of ammo and weapons. We saw no VC, even the ones we knew were there were not visible.

The New Zealand Captain said, "Let's go, our chopper will be here soon. Let's find a good landing zone and pop smoke."

"We have to walk about four miles back," I told him. "Where is your unit?"

"Bien Hoa Air Base. We are Special Forces. We go out

every other night for three months, and then we go home. We have an ear contest going on with the other guys."

"How did you know those tunnels were there and you flew right to them?"

"We have good S-2 (meaning intelligence). You guys just happened to be the closest to where we were going."

"Glad we could help."

Their chopper came in taking them back to Bien Hoa. We walked back to our unit and opened us up some 1944 C-rations. Jacob came over asking if everything went okay. I said, "Yeah, you didn't blow us up. Relax, if you did, I wouldn't be here to harass you!"

We didn't see much of anything for a couple of weeks. Harlem was anxious about his R&R. He only had 7 or 8 days to go. He never did get much mail, and never received any packages. Bear and I were always getting something. We always shared with him. One evening we were sitting around playing poker with bullets and just messing around when Harlem said, "I should be sending my money to my grandma. My mom has probably been spending it."

"Mine didn't get here until the very last minute. It'll come." I was trying to reassure him, but I talked to Gus and Bear anyway. All together, we had $225.00. We decided if his money didn't come, we'd give it to him. I gathered up a little more without him knowing it.

Bear said, "Let's give it to him so he can go. His money ain't coming." That night in our APC, Bear, Harlem and I started talking. We gave him the money. He almost cried.

"I know my money ain't coming. It'll take a long time to pay you back."

Bear replied, "This ain't no loan. We can't use it, and it's your turn to get out of here for a while."

"I've lived my whole life in Harlem, never really knowing any white people. The only thing I ever got from any of them was this war. I've never taken anything from a white man.

I've fought with you, for you, ate and slept with you, and Bear, I didn't even like you for a long time. I do want out of here for a while. I will take it. Thank you . . . ain't we somethin' . . . Okie, Texan, and Harlem . . . three amigos!"

"I wrote my grandma about you guys, but I never told her you were white. I'm writing her and telling her what you did. My money is going to start going to her. She's a good woman, but never had much use for white people. I know if I get out of here and go back to Harlem, I'll never have another relationship like I have now as long as I live. I will always know that at least you two and Rex are really human."

"Harlem, that's enough. Just have a good time."

Harlem finally got to leave for Singapore. That left just me and Bear in our APC. I asked Sgt. Hines if we were going to get anybody else. "I don't know."

"Well, can you find out? It's a little hard with just two of us."

"I'll see."

We knew he wouldn't. He was afraid to talk to the Captain. We still weren't doing much. Sgt. Hines said, "Will you go to Headquarters FDC and man the radio tonight?"

"Yeah, I guess."

"Jacob is by himself, and he's tired."

"Okay." I went over there, leaving Bear by himself. I plotted the targets. The storms had been so strong we weren't sending anybody out on Patrol. We were in a flat area that flooded 6 to 8 inches every night. There was no contact on the radio, so I sat down in a metal folding chair and put my foot on the radio mount inside the APC. They were using some kind of generator outside to keep the radios and lights going. The canvas extensions, when connected to each other, provided black out conditions on the outside. I was leaning back in that metal chair trying to stay awake. There was 6 inches of water on the ground so no one was moving around much. I started writing a letter to keep awake.

Then it happened. An RPG round (that was the round fired from a bamboo barrel that would penetrate the exterior of a tank) hit the side of the APC. It hit the back of the radio and radio mount; shrapnel went everywhere. The radio had blocked it from hitting me in the face. The fire was bright orange. The radio shorted out. I tried to pull my foot from the mount. The fire looked like a lightning bolt going to my foot. The metal plate in my boot was conducting the electrical short, deadening my left leg. All the hair was gone, and the sole of my boot started to stink. I finally got my foot loose and out of that metal chair. I rolled down the APC ramp and went into the water. I couldn't feel anything. A Major from S-2 intelligence came and dragged me out of the water and on to a table they had set up. Most of my feeling came back quickly, except for my left leg. The medic kept sticking needles into it, and I couldn't feel it. Captain Dales came up and said, "We need to medevac him out of here."

I lay there soaking wet, and the storm was still really strong. The Major told them to get a cot to lay me down on. "We can't get a chopper in here right now."

The medic said, "I'll get Captain Baker to look at him."

"Who's that?"

"The squadron doctor."

"I didn't know we had one." He came and looked at me and told Base Camp to take my records to the First Aid tent, and they would fly me to Base Camp as soon as they could. He said my foot was blistered, but I couldn't feel it. I asked him if that was the only round we took.

"No, there were some more, but you are the only one hurt." It continued to storm into the next morning. The Doctor gave me something to help me sleep. It didn't stop raining until about 10:00 A.M. The feeling was coming back in my leg, but not my foot. Bear brought me some cookies that we had stashed.

"Old Hines 57 just told me what happened."

"Yeah, I came over here and work in a more secure area and find a way for something to happen."

"Are they going to medevac you?"

"I doubt it now. The feeling is coming back. I'll be able to ride in an APC. The doctor asked me what I wanted to do." I told him, "Stay, I'll be okay." Bear and Jacob helped me back to my APC, trying to keep my foot out of the water and mud.

Bear said, "Now we got one man and a cripple to run this APC. Well, at least we shouldn't have to go on any patrols for a few days, maybe until Harlem gets back."

"Bear, you need to put in for your R&R before long."

"I'm going to Australia if I have to wait six months. I want to go there or Hawaii, but the married men should go first," he told me. I thought about how hard it was for me to leave Bangkok, just knowing what I had to come back to. How in the world can they have the courage to leave their wives, knowing what was ahead of them?"

I just couldn't face that kind of decision. I didn't want to be close to anyone. I thought I would only bring more pain to someone I loved. I really had no one to talk to. I was 10,000 miles away from home in a place that I never expected to leave alive. How could I possibly try to figure out my future?

My foot began to heal, and in about four days, all the feeling had come back. The raw meat from the burns hurt, but I didn't do much walking. I could handle it. There weren't too many men where I was complaining about the conditions, so I kept my feelings to myself.

Sgt. Hines showed up, asking me if I had written home. "Yeah, a couple of times."

He said, "You should write more often than that."

"You mean, since I got hurt?"

"Did you tell them about getting hurt?"

"Well, no, why would I do that?"

"The 1st Sergeant had your family notified that you were medevacked to Base Camp for a leg injury."

"Why would he do that? We never write what happens and then these idiots tell them?"

"Yeah, you better write to them and tell them what happened."

We had a 1st Sergeant that's too scared to come to the field, telling my family what happened to me. "I'm surprised you had the guts to tell me! Are you and the 1st Sgt. brothers, or are you just both stupid?"

"You shouldn't talk to me that way in front of other troops."

"Well, you shouldn't be in my APC. There's a loaded M-16 in here!"

He left pretty quick. I had to try and write a letter describing what happened. It made me sick. Bear started laughing. I told him, "This ain't funny!"

"I know, I've just never seen you mad before. Ole' Hines 57 thought you were going to shoot him, and I wasn't real sure you weren't."

"Sometimes I don't understand how there can be so many jackasses in one place who are supposed to be my leaders."

"You need to take a pain pill and relax."

"I can't!!! I've got to write a letter!" I tried to explain things the best I could, letting them know I didn't know the Army had notified them. I went through all of that, and then their letter back told me they were never notified. I didn't know who to be mad at—I guess the Army.

Harlem got back from his R&R in Singapore. He thanked us again and said, "I better stay around and take care of you. Your foot looks awful!"

"It looks good now!" Bear told him.

We told Harlem that we hadn't done much since he left, but we felt like something was going on. Jacob wouldn't tell us as Chris had, and Sgt. Hines didn't know anything. We hadn't seen Captain Dales. It was really different around there with Rex and Chris gone.

We stayed there two more days. My foot was almost completely well. I could walk pretty well, but not for a long distances. Captain Dales came and told us of a mission south of where we were. He wanted Harlem and me to be his machine gunners and for me to wear a radio set to call in artillery. "We will need fire support." Captain Dales would stand between us, and his headset would be to direct the troops. He was ready to go, but not in a gung-ho way. He was just a different type of leader. I was honored to work with him. We knew he meant business, but we also could feel his heart of concern for us. We knew the GI was the cheapest and most expendable piece of equipment the Army had, but Captain Dales didn't do things that way. We were important to him.

The philosophy of the war was *attrition nutrition.* We had more men than the enemy and would eventually win for that reason. There were over five hundred fifty thousand men in Vietnam in 1968. We never seemed to have enough to keep our unit up to maximum strength. I also felt our new Commander, Colonel Patton, was trying to do things differently. We weren't going on nearly as many patrols just to be going and losing troops. In addition, when we had 30 days left, we'd go to Base Camp or a rear area. That was evidence enough for me that he cared. What news we did hear from the world always seemed to point to us as lower class draftees, not smart enough to avoid the draft. The ones that joined knew what they were getting into so it was okay if the politicians directed them into slaughter—at least that was the message we were getting. No wonder there was so much turmoil and unrest back in the United States when the ground troops in Vietnam were fighting for their Country and the freedom of the children of South Vietnam.

We would be going into an area that the 25th Infantry had been in about 30 days earlier. Captain Dales told us they had drawn heavy fire, and the VC were well-equipped. Some were regular North Vietnamese Army. The Captain was ready, and I was proud to stand beside him. It was a pretty large operation, so D and A troops were also going. All of us were leaving the perimeter with only C Troop to cover the Howitzers and Headquarters—FDC, the complete perimeter. Our Lt. Col. stayed in Headquarters with a couple of Majors with S-2. The Full Bird Colonel Patton was directing us from the air. Usually our Lt. Col. did that, but Patton was taking charge of this operation.

I checked in with Jacob and got the coordinates ready. I made the FDC aware of what they might need the guns to do. I was actually ready to go. I had sat for two weeks. Time went by so slowly. If I was doing something, even a mission, I wasn't thinking about home. We were told to hang back, be the last troop, and let D Troop lead the way. Captain Marino was tough and a mean guy. He never took any prisoners. He looked mean, and to me, he looked old. He was a big man, just the perfect leader for combat. My choice was still Captain Dales. He used better judgment in taking care of his troops. I remember Captain Dales questioning Colonel Patton about his decision to make us lay back. Patton chewed on him so long and loud that he finally took his headset off. No Captain questioned Colonel Patton.

Captain Marino took off on the trails. They were going every direction. He was a really gung-ho guy. Colonel Patton was directing them from the air. They were drawing fire from everywhere. As a Forward Observer, there was no way I could call in artillery. They were all over the place. Captain Marino didn't want any, anyway. He said, "We'll get them ourselves. Don't be blowing them up." He was exactly that way with or without Patton. He chased VC all over the hill, shooting direct fire at them. We couldn't tell how many were in the area but the firing was heavy in all directions. D Troop and Captain Marino were doing almost the entire mission. A Troop was moving in a different direction, south of D Troop. Patton was directing everything from the air. It sounded bad from where we were. Captain Marino was talking so fast he would talk over the top of Colonel Patton in all the missions and fire fights. This one did seem to be more organized.

We did very little that day but were told we would go

back to the same area the next day, and B Troop would probably take the lead. I wanted so much to hear Captain Marino's reaction when Colonel Patton told him to stay back and let B Troop lead. Captain Dales was the Captain. He was really excited. We had a quiet night. Maybe a few mortars came in, but nothing heavy. Captain Marino had come up with 22 for a body count with no losses. He also said he saw areas he didn't like and believed there were a lot more VC in that area.

Colonel Patton had arranged to have some South Vietnamese Army guys flown in to fight with us. The next morning we were waiting on them to show up. I told Captain Dales, "This is a waste. Those guys are worthless; they'll get us all killed."

Captain Dales said, "This is a Special Force Ranger Group. They won't run. They're well trained." I knew there were some of those guys around. I had just never seen them. We knew Laos had some tough soldiers fighting with us, but politically, they didn't exist. I ended up being anxious for them to show up. Colonel Patton was waiting for the arrival. I still think it was a "feather in your cap" day for some upper brass. When they arrived, they looked ready and anxious to go. Two of them just jumped on our APC. They scattered all over our APCs and tanks. They looked glad to be with us.

We went to almost exactly the same location Captain Marino had gone. We got a little deeper into the jungle, and the world fell in on us. We were hit while A Troop was being hit. It seemed like it was almost a timed hit, which was very unusual. That hardly ever happened. There was no time to think, just shoot. It was impossible to keep our APC turned toward the fire because it was coming from all around us. Colonel Patton landed so we could call in artillery. Captain Dales told me to walk it in, over shoot our position by 500 yards, and walk it closer to us. I was calling for Fire Direction Control. I was calling for fuse delay. We didn't take a chance on it exploding in the air above our heads. Harlem was so big that he had to duck down. I saw some machine gun fire bullets deflecting from the inside of his M-60 shield, meaning they were behind us so we couldn't turn for protection. The ARVN Rangers had scattered all over, but they were fighting and trying to destroy machine gun nests. I was trying to fire my M-60 and call in artillery. It was uncomfortable with three of us back there, especially with so much fire.

I finally got the artillery to an effective distance. I could hear that Captain Marino and D Troop were coming. Captain Dales was doing a great job directing the firefight, and at times, he sounded like Captain Marino. Everyone was proud of him. Harlem and I were doing all we could when an RPG round hit Captain Dales square in the back, a round a foot long, 3" in diameter. It was supposed to explode on impact, but it didn't explode. The round had buried itself into Captain Dales' back. He was lying in the floor of our APC with an unexploded round in his back. Harlem and I both ducked down looking at him and each other. I used my radio to tell FDC what had happened. Harlem was trying to remove Captain Dales' headset so he could talk to Captain Marino. We were trying not to move him any more than we had to. We knew he was dead, but if that shell went off, three more of us would be dead too. We were sweating and nervous. I was supposed to be calling artillery and using an M-60 machine gun. Now we had a dead Captain with a live round in his back. Captain Marino found out what happened. Harlem was trying to talk to him about Captain Dales, telling them he's KIA (killed in action). He kept telling us to get him out of there and move to the rear with him. We never called for a medic. He was dead, and there was no need to endanger anyone else. Harlem said, "Marino wants us back now!"

"Did you tell him I was the Forward Observer?"

He yelled, "Get him out of there, and stop the artillery now!"

I knew he didn't know what we were trying to tell him,

but I told the driver to back us out of there as gently as possible. "How can I do that?"

"Just do the best you can!" We continued to fire our M-60s. It seemed like it took forever for us to get out of there, and it was rough terrain. I didn't know whether to try and hold Captain Dales to prevent him from moving so much. Then Harlem was hit with a .50-caliber round. It hit his flak jacket and knocked him down. The jacket kept it from penetrating Harlem's skin. He was on the floor with Captain Dales. He started to stand up. I told him to hold on to the Captain and just stay down!

A Lieutenant from D Troop had started calling in artillery. We finally made it back to the rear, and here came the doctor (the Captain who had taken care of my foot). He jumped in and saw Captain Dales with that round and said, "He's KIA!"

"I know that."

"Get a mortar man over here to remove that round." An E-6 Sergeant came over and just grabbed the round, threw it, and shot it, exploding it just a few feet away.

"You could have let us get away from here before you did that!"

"What's the difference? We'll all die now or later."

"That's right, but I don't want to die from a Sergeant's stupidity!"

He said, "I handle unexploded ammo all the time. How long you think I'm going to make it?"

Captain Marino had made it up to where we were. He was the .50-caliber machine gunner himself. He again called for the artillery to be shut off. He was going after them. Colonel Patton was back in the air directing the mission. We had all grown to respect and love Captain Dales. I knew that whomever Captain Marino caught was going to suffer in the worst possible way. Harlem and I were told to go back to our APC, where Bear was. We looked at Harlem's chest where the .50-caliber bullet had hit him after a deflection and then hit his flak jacket. It was swollen and sore, and we told him he'd probably be bruised for a while.

Harlem said, "Can you believe what just happened to us again? I've got to tell my grandma about this one and tell her whatever she is doing, to keep it up."

I said, "It's pretty obvious to me that someone is moving on our behalf. I don't really feel anything, but someone is with us." I wasn't thanking Him for watching over me. I was still upset for even being there.

The little ARVN Rangers had killed several VC and brought two to Captain Marino alive. They had some paperwork with them. Bear said, "I don't even want to know what will happen to them." We were still shook up. Gus tried to get us to eat, but we couldn't because of the shell not exploding, because of Harlem getting hit, and also because of losing a Captain who we really had grown to respect and appreciate. Everyone that knew him liked him, privates to majors. I was just sick and kept thinking about his wife and two children.

Gus said, "You and Harlem are covered with Captain Dales' blood!"

"I know, but I am out of clean clothes. If I have to wear someone else's blood besides my own, then it might as well be Captain Dales.'" I had never let anything bother me like the way this did. All I could do is whatever I had to do for four months, still 120 days. I was 'shorter' than Gus, Harlem, and Bear. Gus and Harlem had 150 days, and Bear had 180. The next few days just went by. We were at the lowest point we had been, just existing. I had quit even trying to be tough. Nothing made sense to me, and I didn't care what happened. Some were talking about going back to Base Camp for a week or so. That didn't even lift our spirits. We felt like we were in a deep, dark pit.

Sgt. Hines came over to talk to Gus and me about morale, not just ours, but the whole troop's morale. He said, "These guys are looking to you and Gus to be leaders. They respect you, so try and lift their morale."

"You're the ranking Sergeant. You do something to lift us up. Take us up to Bien Hoa Air Base, get us a movie to watch, get me some clean fatigues, a hot meal, shower, case of beer, YOU do something. I don't have it in me! Send me on a patrol. I can't stand four more months of this. I try and write home telling everyone I'm okay. Well, I'M NOT OKAY!!! Don't be leaning on me; I'm not that strong."

"Sgt., I'm just trying to help, but you're getting loaded down with self-pity. I'll get you some clean clothes and a wet rag to get that blood and smell off of you."

"Get some for me and Harlem too!" Gus yelled. Gus started talking to Harlem about his R&R, trying to break the mood. It worked. Bear was still set on Australia. In a few minutes, Sgt. Hines came back with clean clothes, socks, and a wet rag for Harlem and me.

I said, "Thank you, Sgt."

He walked off and Gus looked at me, "I figured you'd chew on him some more."

I wanted to ask him why we didn't get this stuff three days ago, but I'd said enough. "There are a lot of guys leaving here and going to a 'crazy house.' I don't want to leave that way."

"It must be something about ole' 'Hines 57.' That's twice you unloaded on him."

Sgt. James and Rex deserved and earned my respect, but Hines was scared to go on Patrol. He wasn't a leader, and I just plain didn't respect the man. "Guess I do have to quit making it so obvious."

CHAPTER 10

COWBOY LING

Jesus said, "Let the little children come to me, and do not hinder them, for the kingdom of heaven belongs to such as these." Matthew 19:14

B Troop was getting to be a mess—no Captain and a 1st Sergeant who wouldn't go into the field. My immediate Sgt. E-6 would not go on Patrol, but we were getting more organized on top with Colonel Patton, but now it seemed the bottom was unraveling.

In a few more days, we left that place, going past where Captain Dales lost his life. We were still one man short on our APC. Hines told us another new guy would be coming in a few days. Bear had been the driver longer than he should have been, but he never complained. He had changed so much since he first came. He never bragged or complained. We all liked him. We went through a village somewhere near Ben Cat. White phosphorous bombs had burned just a few hundred yards from the village. There were small children running beside us, asking for food. They were dirty with black smut from playing around the bomb craters and burned areas. We were throwing out C-rations when all of a sudden the convoy stopped. We had never stopped in a village before. I was just hoping we weren't getting in a firefight or that someone in front of us hadn't ran over a mine. Captain Marino, of all people, had ordered us to stop. He said,

"Let's get out and walk around. We need a refresher course on why we are here."

His medicine was exactly what we needed. None of us could believe that it was Captain Marino who had ordered it. We held those kids, took pictures, and gave them all we had. A little boy with a cowboy hat caught my eye. He told me his name was Cowboy Ling, probably 5 or 6 years old. He smiled so bright—I put his hat on and let him wear mine. It felt good. I was very close to some of my younger cousins. I was so thankful they were in the U.S.A.

Gus yelled at me. He wanted me to see two little girls. They were twins, cute as they could be. They reminded me so much of my cousin Kelly; she had written to me. Those kids penetrated my heart as nothing ever had. I wanted so much to get them out of there. God had shown me three little hearts, three reasons I was there . . . enough to keep me strong and doing what I was there for. Harlem had tears in his eyes. He said, "These kids don't have a chance. Their mother was trying to sell herself while you were taking their pictures. I just gave her what money I had. Where I'm from, I've seen what drugs do to people, destroying their lives, but I haven't seen nothing like this." Those kids brought understanding back into our hearts. That's why we were there and so many were dying.

We hated to leave them, but we were lifted in Spirit. It was worth taking that thirty minutes to do that. It was like the darkness had lifted, and God had let His light shine on all of us. My granny's saying came back to me, "God won't put more on you than you can stand." I knew it had to be someone as powerful as God to get Captain Marino to stop that convoy and get some of the load off of us.

We were traveling closer to our Base Camp. No one said where we were going. It was flatter terrain and easier to travel. We made camp in an area only about ten miles from Base Camp. It brought our hopes up some. We were really dirty and tired and wanted some hot food. We learned that evening that Colonel

Patton had relieved our Lieutenant Colonel of his command. Captain Marino was given a field promotion to Major but would remain as Troop Commander. We had no patrols that night and didn't receive any mortar attacks.

The next morning we received word that we were going back to the Black Horse Base Camp. All of our equipment needed servicing, we needed supplies, and we had many things to do that we had neglected while out in the field.

CHAPTER 11
NEW OFFICERS

There is a time for everything, and a season for every activity under heaven. a time to be born and a time to die, a time to plant and a time to uproot, a time to kill and a time to heal, a time to tear down and a time to build, a time to weep and a time to laugh . . . a time to love and a time to hate, a time for war and a time for peace. Ecclesiastes 3:1–4,8

Gus asked me, "Are you going to go to Headquarters?"

"I don't know. Hines or Jacob either one know I've been doing that, so maybe I won't have to." We took showers, got haircuts, ate hot meals from the Mess Hall, started doing Maintenance, and here came Sgt. Hines.

"We have a new Lieutenant Colonel." I thought for sure I was going back to Headquarters to work with Jacob and whomever else they had over there, but Hines was saying our new Colonel wanted ambush patrols around Base Camp. We had guard duty around the perimeter in bunkers (10 x 10, two men in each one), mines buried, and constantina wire around the complete Base Camp.

"Why go on an ambush patrol outside the perimeter?"

Hines said, "I don't know, just get one together for tonight. We got four new guys. We'll give one to you. He'll be here in a few minutes."

"Where's he from?"

"I don't know."

We saw him walking across Base Camp looking for our APC. He looked lily white and scared to death. He walked up to Harlem, asking if this is where he was supposed to be. Harlem said that guy from Oklahoma is the Tank Commander. I was just a few feet away. Every time I saw new guys, I thought of the way I was just a few months earlier so I tried not to mess with them too much. I just tried to make them feel comfortable. I had Bear show him where to put his gear and where our hooch was while at Base Camp. I was washing my clothes in a large ammo can when they came back. I said, "You know how to drive an APC?"

"Yes, Sir."

"You do?"

"I drove one at Ft. Hood in my training."

"You mean we got someone that knows how to drive and was trained on an APC? Where are you from?"

"Boston."

"Boston? I've never met anyone from Boston. Harlem is from New York City, Bear is from Texas, and I am from Oklahoma."

"Yes, Sir. I'm glad to meet you."

"What's your name?"

"Chester."

"Chester? That doesn't sound like a Boston name."

"Well, it's Chester, Sir."

"You keep calling me Sir. Quit that! I don't care for it."

"Yes, Sir."

I looked at Bear and he was laughing. "What did you tell him?"

"Just that you were a Captain!"

"Chester, I'm an E-5 Sergeant, so call me Sgt., okay?"

We needed a laugh. "Just take it easy. We got plenty to do, and any of us will help you. Just ask if you need something."

Harlem asked, "Were you drafted?"

"No, I joined for three years."

"Did you volunteer for 'Nam?"

"No, Sir, I just got sent here. I've been in the Army for five months."

"We all came here after five months, and Chester, I'm not a Sir, either. I'm just an E-4, okay?"

"You're just so big; I just called you sir."

"You called me sir 'cause I'm a big black guy? That's so weird! Where I come from, everyone else would be sir."

Chester would get nervous and talk real fast, and with his accent, we couldn't understand him. Bear said, "I don't think Chester will be a radio operator."

He became more comfortable with us and started letting Bear show him about the APC so he could become our driver. Bear said, "This guy already knows more than I did."

Harlem laughed, "You didn't know nothin,' man!" Bear had just talked as if he knew something.

I was trying to go over in my mind about a Patrol . . . ten men. It was usually twelve. I just hoped I got ten volunteers. I knew I was going, and Gus, Harlem, and Bear would always go. I didn't want Chester to have to go his first day.

We went on Patrol with all volunteers. We all felt like it was the dumbest thing we had ever done, but we just went. They took us out on an APC and dumped us 600 yards from Base Camp. We squatted down. Gus said, "You think we sneaked up on 'em?"

"I don't know who is running things, but we are in a hurt for leadership. We are like sitting ducks." I was told to radio check every hour. "Yeah, I can do that quietly!" I turned the volume way down and made a couple of radio checks, then told Jacob, "I'm not doing this all night. I'll call if we see or need anything!"

About three hours went by, and I could hear someone on the radio yelling at me. I answered. It was our new Lieutenant Colonel telling me he ordered me to radio check every hour.

Yeah, I needed to do that! (Six hundred yards from Base Camp, and I was radio checking!) We never did that in the field. I told him the radio wasn't working correctly, and I was trying to save the battery in case we needed it.

Gus said, "He'll probably want to check out your radio."

"Okay, I know how to loosen a fuse."

We sat there all night, just taking turns sleeping. When the sun came up, I turned the radio up louder. I asked, "Do we walk back or is an APC coming to get us?"

"We'll send an APC after you."

"Okay, we'd like to get there in time for breakfast." We stood up as we saw the APC coming and started walking toward the road. Then they ran over a mine, blowing the track off on the opposite side of the driver. It was also a low charge mine, which prevented the driver from being killed. It was an old mine that just decided to explode.

We walked on back, and the track was being towed. We missed breakfast, but the cook kept some back for us. Here came Hines yelling, "The First Sergeant wants you to report to him."

"Can I eat first?"

"I don't know. I guess so!"

It didn't take much for me to go off, especially after being sent out on such a stupid mission. We were still in range of our own perimeter fire and then the mine. We were lucky that we didn't get someone killed. I reported to the First Sgt. and told him exactly what went on and what we were ordered to do. We still didn't have our own Captain, but Major Marino was heading into the door. He was mad. I thought it was over the radio deal. I told him what happened on Patrol.

"Who told you to go outside our perimeter 600 yards?"

"I don't know. Hines told me, but I talked to the new Lt. Col. on the radio last night."

"You did?"

"Yes, Sir. I'm sure it was him." He asked me if I was the guy that had been with Captain Dales.

"Yes, Sir. I was."

He walked right over to me and raised his arm. I almost ducked. He put his arm on my shoulder. "I was proud of you guys. You handled a tough deal correctly."

"Thank you, Sir."

"I'll find out what goof sent you out there! Colonel Patton is hot about it."

Our new Lt. Col. lasted three days. He was relieved of his command. We were running way short on officers. We managed to stay in Base Camp for three weeks getting everything ready to go. Gus and I went to the airport to pick up some new troops. We took the Executive Officer's jeep. It went about 45 - 50 mph. It felt so good. We were acting like kids again. We got to the canopied pavilion to get our guys. They told us to pick up their gear and load it on the jeep. We laughed. They had their rain jackets on covering their rank.

They were First Lieutenants. "We're not used to being laughed at."

"We couldn't see your rank. We need some officers. All ours have been killed. We don't keep them very long!" We had some fun with them on the way back.

I asked, "Did you get drafted?"

"Yeah. Where are you from?"

"I'm from Oklahoma. Where are you from, Sir?"

"I'm from California. I was a stockbroker before I got drafted." At that time in my life, I'd never heard of a stockbroker, so I asked him about it.

"What's that?"

"Son, I'm a gambler."

"Well, you came to the right place. We gamble every day—with our lives."

The other Lieutenant was from Nevada. Gus asked, "You a gambler too?"

"Yeah, I guess."

The California Lieutenant's name was Cotton. He was going to take Captain Dales' place. He was due to make Captain in about thirty days, and Lieutenant Whitney was our new Executive Officer. Major Marino was going to run the squadron—just made Major and was going to do a Lt. Colonel's job. He and Patton had something going. I don't know if they served together before or not, but they clicked and made everything easier for all of us. Gus said, "Now if we had a Sergeant, we'd be back to normal around here."

"Forget that. We've got Hines, and we're shorter than he is, so we're stuck with him." We stayed almost ten more days before we left again. I remember it being around ninety days total that I had left to be over there. We stayed in Base Camp longer than we ever had, but we needed it and enjoyed it. Sgt. Hines got us an old Cary Grant movie from somewhere. Lt. Cotton was Captain Cotton, and Lt. Whitney was our new XO. We had a full crew. We felt pretty good. Chester was a great driver. He could turn so smooth that we wouldn't fall all over the APC. Bear was a machine gunner. He had wanted to be for a long time, but drove without complaining. Harlem was the other M-60 machine gunner, and I was the Tank Commander, .50-caliber machine gunner, and had a headset to talk to Chester on. It seemed like forever since Rex had talked to me back when I was trying to drive. Major Marino was running our squadron, and Colonel Patton was the Regimental Commander.

Everything seemed so much better, except we were going back to the Iron Triangle. We all knew we would be either in Cambodia or extremely close to it. I don't know if it was the *name* "Iron Triangle" or if it really *was* the darkest and most brutal place that I had ever been. We weren't looking forward to going back. It was a place where we could find nothing good. We knew we were going to lose troops. Even today, I can read that kind of hopelessness in Veteran's eyes. It's a look we all had, except for Chester, but we knew that in just a few days he would look the same as us. He was always smiling or trying to say something funny or uplifting over the headset as we were traveling. I didn't have much response except to tell him to pay attention and keep his eyes open. "I lost a track in this same area eight months ago."

"Okay, Sgt."

"I'm just nervous."

"I know you are, and you're a lot better driver than I was. We'll be okay." I was concerned about Captain Cotton and Lt. Whitney, being their first trip to the field, especially the Iron Triangle, but I also felt good about Major Marino being in charge of our squadron.

We weren't doing anything different from before, except the Mess Trailer was with us, meaning we might get a hot meal once a day, and we'd probably be there for a while. We set up in the same place we were before, next to the Cambodian border. Captain Cotton told us to dig in. I said, "Sir, this is the rainy season. They'll fill up with water before we get them dug."

"Use your ponchos for canvas to cover them, but dig in."

"Yes, Sir." We dug in the mud, and they filled with water.

In just a short while, Captain Cotton came over looking for Hines. He said, "I need a patrol for tonight."

"Sir, Gus and I always do that. Sgt. Hines never goes."

"Why not?"

"He's scared, I guess."

"It's his job, and I'll make him go!"

"Sir, it's okay. He's worthless to us and might get someone killed. He's not what we need. We can do better without him. Sir, I am the Forward Observer and radio operator. If you think we need someone else, okay, but don't give me Hines. If you want to go, we'll be happy to take you."

"I'm not scared to go, but it's not my job or what I need to be doing right now. Just tell me how many men to take."

"Ten or twelve . . . okay, Sir, we will be ready." As difficult and dangerous as it was to go on patrol, Gus and I never had any trouble getting volunteers. They knew our situation, and we really didn't want to make them go. We had a bunch of good men. War had turned some young boys into good men. None of us were 21 yet, and none of us could even vote back home—yet we could fight and even lose our lives for our Country. Some things just really didn't make much sense.

Gus, as always, took the point, an extra step he didn't have to take but did every time. We walked pretty deep into the jungle, expecting any second to draw fire. We could feel them moving, and I knew there were tunnels under us. We set our perimeter with claymore mines and lay in the wet grass trying to slap mosquitoes without making noise. We took malaria pills every day. Those mosquitoes were large and would draw blood every time they bit you. Chester's bright white skin just attracted them. I could hear him rolling around. Some black ants were also biting us. The rain came down hard. It was a tremendous storm with lightning everywhere. It would tingle the ground as we lay there. When the lightning would flash, we could see several yards and saw nothing. At least we felt better about that. We made it through the night with no firefight and no mortars.

As we walked back, drenched with our boots sloshing from all the water, I looked at Chester. He looked like a solid red bump. "Have you got something on?"

"What do you mean?"

"Deodorant or aftershave?"

"Yeah, both!"

"You don't wear that out here. That's one reason you were eaten up last night!"

"Nobody told me that, Sgt."

"I'm sorry. You're the one hurting. Get some salve from the medic."

We got back, hoping the sun would shine long enough to dry us out. The mail came. I always got a lot of mail and a package every month. My family took turns mailing me a food package. We always shared it. Harlem very seldom got mail. When he did, it was almost always from his grandma. I looked over at Chester. He had a ton of mail. "You got a big family?"

"Yeah, I got six brothers and sisters and lots of cousins."

I went through the routine of telling him what to write home and to burn his mail after he read it. "I've been told that a couple of times already."

"You'll probably be told some more."

Bear got quite a bit of mail also. His grandma had sent him a large printed Bible verse. He asked if he could put it up in the APC.

"Sure you can." It was 1John 15:13. **"Greater love has no one than this, that he lay down his life for his friends."** She added . . . **or his Country.**

Harlem said, "We probably should have had a Scripture in here all the time."

I asked Bear, "You got people praying for you?"

"Some do every day, and some do sometimes. I wrote and told them about the night we saw the Southern Cross. Now, they're all writing me about Jesus."

Harlem said, "That's okay. We need Him with us."

Captain Cotton walked over and told Bear his R&R came through for Australia. He got Sydney. "Yep, you can leave in two weeks. You can go to Base Camp in seven days."

"I'm ready. I've already had my money sent and some clothes too."

We had things pretty good for a couple of days. We had a hot meal every day, and the VC weren't doing anything but mortaring us for a few minutes and then leaving. D Troop (Major Marino's old troop) was going out on patrol. They had a 1st Lt. who Marino was training, and he was going on Patrol every night to learn what it was. He was new in country and had Major Marino to teach him. He was another Italian like Marino and turned out to be pretty good. He wanted to be career Army so he couldn't afford to mess up. Colonel Patton kept telling us there was going to be a large VC troop movement coming down from Cambodia going to Saigon. We were also told that if we caught them in Cambodia, we could call in artillery, just like we didn't know we were there. That was one thing about Marino. He didn't care much for politics, and with Patton, he seemed more eager to go after them. Everyone knew that they would hit and run back to Cambodia, so it was going to be a big shock to them when we went after them. After about five days, there still wasn't much happening. Marino decided to go in the daytime and to go on more search and destroy missions.

CHAPTER 12

CAMBODIA

You will live in constant suspense, filled with dread both night and day, never sure of your life. In the morning you will say, "If only it were evening!" and in the evening, "If only it were morning!"—because of the terror that will fill your hearts and the sights that your eyes will see. Deuteronomy 28:66–67

We got word we would be going west the next day (B and D Troops). West meant straight into Cambodia. We were going to find the VC. Patton wanted large body counts, and we were going to find them. I told Hines that Bear only had one day before his R&R, and he didn't need to go with us. "You'll be one man short."

"We've been one man short most of the time."

"I don't think I can allow that!"

"Sgt. Hines, he's not going. He would go, he's not afraid to go, but I'm saying he's not going! If you don't want us to be one man short, I'll talk to Captain Cotton, and you can ride with us and start doing your job. You have stood by and *watched* your whole time over here. I'll bet you have written home telling your family what all you've done. Either leave me alone, or you'll go to the jungle with us."

Surprisingly enough, Bear stayed back, and we went one man short. We went deep into Cambodia. I was somewhat worried about our artillery being able to support us with Marino always wanting to make blood. I was trying hard to figure our position on the map. It didn't go very far into Cambodia, and I knew we were off the map. Captain Cotton kept asking me where we were. I would give him our last map coordinates and then add our direction and distance the best I could. We got to an edge of a rubber plantation and stopped and then pulled off on both sides of the road. My guess was we were about three miles into Cambodia. We still had not drawn fire. Marino said, "Let's shake them up. We can't get air support in Cambodia, so use artillery. Call some in."

I called Captain Cotton, telling him where I thought we were. He said, "Shoot five miles, which should be two miles over us, then walk it back." I did that.

As we waited, Captain Cotton asked me, "You been to college?"

I was nervous and wasn't going to listen to that college boy stuff again. "No, just an Okie who got drafted." It got completely silent. We heard the shells going over our heads whistling loudly. They landed about a thousand yards in front of us, a lot closer than I had thought.

Captain Cotton said, "Good Gosh, I got an E-5 Okie Sgt. calling artillery in over my head!"

"You told me you were a gambler. You'll have something to write home about." I looked over at Chester, and his eyes could not have been open any wider. He still was bright white. He looked so young . . . only had two or three whiskers.

We shot for over two hours, and then we started moving in. Captain Cotton asked, "Did you shut off the artillery?"

"Yeah, I think I did—you go first!" It was fun messing with him, but I knew it was time to stop.

We traveled right into a sophisticated Ho Chi Minh trail. The jungle was so dense. They had a road in the jungle that could not be seen from the air. They had traveled with carts, and we had to drive right into it to find it. Patton still couldn't see it from the air, but we were driving east, right back to Vietnam.

The trail was so clear that we didn't have to bust jungle. We had about sixteen APCs and six tanks. The VC used the road so regularly that we weren't worried about mines, but we couldn't see five feet on either side of us, and we were expecting to draw fire at any time. We just kept going. Once in a while, we popped smoke so Patton knew where we were. By the looks of the trail, it was being used regularly and recently.

Marino said, "They have already moved around us. Just stay on the trail. Shoot sporadic fire once in a while into the dense jungle." It felt like a sauna. The sweat was in our eyes, and we couldn't see. The diesel fumes from our vehicles were so thick it was hard to breathe. The canopy of trees and jungle was so tight that the fumes just hung in the air. It was almost as if we were in a closed building. I had a rag on my forehead and a rag on my mouth.

Chester remarked, "This is so weird. I haven't seen any birds. I'm kind of into that."

"I've been here 290 days, and I've never seen a bird, so bird watching may be difficult around here."

We just kept moving deeper down the road, still completely camouflaged. We expected to start drawing fire any time. Colonel Patton told us there was an opening in the jungle about 100 yards ahead. We approached the opening, hoping to get some air. We all went outside the jungle road and saw no tracks of where the cart trails went. Patton ordered us off the tracks, except for one man to search the area. There had to be some tunnels. It took just a few minutes to find such a large tunnel. It was almost five feet deep. We could almost stand up. There were air vent holes every few feet made with bamboo. We found some old ammo and some paperwork. Some of the papers were American letters—none in our unit. We always burned our mail so the VC couldn't get our names.

The tunnels started splitting off into smaller ones. I wasn't eager to start searching them. I had been in only a few, and I had refused once to go into one that was half-full of water.

I got into a situation where I had to go or ask someone else to do something that I wouldn't do. My dad and his brothers and my grandpa had all been coal miners at one time. I had an uncle who came to America as a small boy from Yugoslavia. He still worked in the coal mines of Southeastern Oklahoma. I had felt his knees several years before, and they were solid calluses where he crawled into the mines to work. He worked hard all of his life. He had written me a letter saying how proud he was of me and how proud he was to live in America. My Aunt told me she never knew of him writing a letter to anyone else. She said, "We lost one nephew over there, and now two more are there." I thought of him as I crawled through the tunnels looking for VC, ammo, or whatever. I just hoped it came out into the larger tunnel. *If I die in here, no one would ever find me.*

I finally saw an air vent and some light coming through it. As I got to it, I could see the larger tunnel again. I hurried over to it to get to where I could see and almost stand up. I could hear Gus talking in front of me, saying the exit was just ahead. It came out in the jungle again. We got to the exit and started getting out when they opened up on us with machine gun fire and AK47s, and we could hear mortars coming out of the tubes. I didn't have a radio. Gus had taken it when I went into the small tunnel. I didn't know where we were anyway. Using the VC tunnel for protection, it seemed like there was just a small platoon of VC firing at us, and it seemed to be in one place. The jungle was so thick that we couldn't throw a hand grenade. We had some grenade launchers, which seemed to be our best bet in taking them out. Marino wanted a flamethrower. I was glad we didn't have one. I heard someone call for a medic. I knew we had good protection, and I didn't know how someone could be hit. It didn't seem to take long to wipe out the small group of VC. I think there were eight.

We got to where our Corporal was. He had fallen into a pit of bamboo stakes with poison on the end. He was a mess. I don't know how he was able to even yell Medic. It took us forever to get him out of there. When we finally got him out and into a body bag, we dragged the dead VC over to the pit and threw them in, blew up the tunnels, and went back to camp, calling in a chopper to take our KIA back to Base Camp. Bear was able to ride it back without waiting until the next morning.

He was excited and ready to go. We were excited for him. Harlem said, "I never thought I'd say this when Bear first came, but I already miss him."

"Yeah, me too. Not to mention the fact that we are in the Iron Triangle and a man short again." We went out day after day, not finding much of anything. We still were getting a hot meal every day. It was a bad area. We were just not finding much enemy activity. Bear was back and had a great time. He was hoping we would be out of the Iron Triangle. Everyone was getting tired and anxious. I was thankful that we weren't finding much. My days were getting shorter. I was thinking about Sgt. James, Rex, and all the ones I was close to that made it out of there.

We went back to Bien Hoa Air Base, enjoyed their Base a lot, and didn't have much to do. They had a laundry service. I took all my old fatigues and got them washed and cleaned. They had a regular barber. I was legal now to go to the NCO Club. I saw a couple of movies and looked up my buddy, Jake, who I was in training with at Ft. Sill. All my time in country, I had never had it as good as I did then.

CHAPTER 13

37 DAYS

I have been deprived of peace; I have forgotten what prosperity is. So I say, "My splendor is gone and all that I had hoped for from the Lord."

I remember my affliction and my wandering, the bitterness and the gall. I will remember them, and my soul is downcast within me. Yet this I call to mind and therefore I have hope: Because of the Lord's great Love we are not consumed, for his compassions never fail. Lamentations 3:17–22

I remember writing a letter home and putting the number 37 on it. That's the day I remembered thinking so clearly . . . I might just make it out of here. It might happen. I had never had that feeling the other 328 days. Everything started to change in my head. How was I going to handle this newfound possibility? It just didn't seem real. All my thoughts were changing. The Big Red One came in and set up beside us. We knew we would be leaving in a few days.

That night I was sleeping on a cot in a tent, and I heard a tank start up in the motor pool. It was coming down the road with three or four guys with loaded M-16s on it, and it was making big circles around the 1st Infantry Division Camp area. Our guys and their guys had a fight in the EM Club. I could hear Captain Cotton yelling, trying to stop the tank. The driver was really drunk. The Red One thought he was going to run over their tents. A group of about twenty 11th Cavalry guys came walking down the road, yelling and talking back and forth, when a grenade went off and shrapnel started tearing holes in our tent. I was running as fast as I could. *Now my own guys are going to kill me.* What a mess that deal turned out to be!

Patton decided very quickly to get us back into the field. I was short enough that I was going back to Base Camp. No more field for me. I had plenty of time to tell Gus, Harlem, Bear, and Chester how proud I was to serve with them. They were really great guys. I knew that Gus and Harlem were just 60 days from home, and Bear had 90 to go. I was thinking how good a cheeseburger, fries, and a cherry coke sounded.

I did whatever at Base Camp—mail, supplies, and guard duty. I was down to nine days when a Major came to me telling me that he needed three men to drive three 5-ton trucks to our Unit in the field. "They are only about fifteen miles from here, but we couldn't fly any to them today, and they need ammo."

I said, "Sir, I've got only nine days left. Colonel Patton said no more field duty for me, so I am not going."

"I can't find anyone else. Patton's not here, so get ready to go."

"Sir, I'm not going!"

"What rank are you?" he asked.

"I'm Sgt. E-5."

"How could they have made a mistake like that? Your unit is in trouble, and you are going. If not, we have a stockade for you, Sgt.!"

"Will I have a shotgun rider?"

"No! Three men for three trucks . . . that's all I could find! The trucks are loaded full of 155 howitzer ammunition."

"Sir, I know it doesn't matter, but I've never driven a 5-ton truck before."

"It's just like a 2.5-ton truck, only easier." I wasn't about to say I'd never driven one of those either! He said there were some South Vietnamese Army guys on patrol so to watch for them. That really made me feel better.

We took off and drove those trucks as fast as we possibly could. It was already dark when we got there, and the gun bunnies unloaded the shells.

I saw all the guys that I hadn't seen in almost a month. Gus tried to get us to stay and go back in the morning. He said, "We've got a cot and tent set up." Captain Cotton asked me why I was out there. He knew how short I was, and he couldn't believe I was there.

I told him, "The new Major was going to put me in jail if I didn't come, but we are going back tonight. Besides that," I added sarcastically, "the South Vietnamese are guarding the road, so I'll be safe."

We left as quickly as we could, bouncing all over the road. How could I have ever made it without God and his shield of protection? We got back and went to bed in our hooches. My buddies were in a tough area, but it seemed we had always been.

The next morning the 1st Sergeant came in and told me to go to the LZ (Landing Zone) and get four body bags from our Unit. He told me my Unit had received some mortars last night hitting in the middle of a tent killing all of them. I asked him who it was. I felt so sick inside. I was asking God to please not let it be one of my brothers.

I arrived just as they were dragging them out, just letting them flop on the ground. "Can't you just lay them down?"

"Ah, they don't feel nothin,'" the guy told me.

"Well, I do! Those guys gave their lives. You better treat them with respect!" They laid them down a few feet from the Landing Zone. I walked over to look at the tags. My worst fear hit me hard when I saw Gus's name on one of the bags. He was one of the four or five best friends I ever had, my "brother." Some Lieutenant told me to unzip the body bag and identify him. I had put so many guys into body bags. I didn't want to see

Gus that way. I wanted to remember him the way he was. He only had about 35 days left, only five more out in the field. I was just devastated trying to understand it. I knew that the smartest and most logical thing I could have done the night before was to have spent the night in Gus's tent and not to drive back at night. It was so dangerous, no shotgun rider . . . just me in a 5-ton truck! I couldn't have been a bigger target! Once again, someone moved on my behalf.

Gus was really a great guy. We had been together for so long. I wrote his mother telling her as much as I could. I could never understand why so many good guys had to die, even my cousin. I've felt guilty all my life that I made it when so many of my "brothers" did not.

I don't understand how God works. Even now, I go to my Combat Vietnam Veterans' group, and we all still carry so much guilt. We can't even talk about some of it to each other, but our eyes tell the stories that are buried down deep inside of us. God is working through me writing this, but I still don't and can't talk about it. My oldest son was reading a book about Vietnam just the other day. I could answer yes or no to some of his questions, but if I tried to talk of an experience, I would just sit and cry. I could not say a word.

I went back to our hooch and gathered up all of Gus's things. I could find some of our R&R pictures and pictures we took in the villages with the little girls and a picture of Cowboy Ling. I had some pictures of a Montagnard Indian tribe. Gus, Harlem, Rex, and I had gotten lost on patrol together. A little Indian man fed us and led us back to our unit. That was so obviously God, but I never realized it at the time.

I mailed Gus's mother everything I could find. Gus was the only child. His mother and father had to somehow live the rest of their lives without their only son. Gus's father was a career Army man, and Gus wanted so much to please him. One cannot do more than give his life.

Four more days, and I was going home. I took all of the

tests for all kinds of diseases. If you had anything wrong, you couldn't go home until you were well. They always said or did something to try and make you worry, but I got cleared pretty quickly and loaded up my things. I got to the airport and saw quite a few of my buddies from AIT in Ft. Sill—Jake, Mike, me, and another guy named Mike from Wisconsin. I looked at that same pavilion I had gone to when I first got there, only this time I was going home. The new guys were getting off the plane to stay their tour. There was the First Aid tent—guys with arms and legs gone, a Captain with an eye patch, guys still on gurneys, and those endless piles of body bags. I was pretty sure Gus was already sent home, but you never knew because it had taken my cousin a week longer than it should have. I thought how ironic it would be if Gus was on the same plane that I was going home on. I should have been happy and excited about going home—a trip I was convinced earlier that I would never make.

I didn't know how to react to anything. I knew I would be welcomed by my family, but I wondered how I would act or feel. How would I ever get rid of this guilt and incredible sadness? I was supposed to go home and be "normal" again. How could I hide my feelings? I knew it was going to take more strength than I felt like I had at that time. I had to be a man, though—my own island, keep to myself, not let anything show. I was proud of my service in Vietnam and the way I handled everything that was expected of me.

We boarded the plane after we greeted the new guys who were getting off, remembering so vividly how we had felt a year earlier, knowing some of them would never go home—except the way Gus did. There is no way to express what I was feeling for those guys and what I knew faced them in Vietnam.

It was a long flight. We stopped again in Japan and then started our trip back to the world. My mind was on Gus. I didn't know anything about where Bear, Harlem, and Chester were or what they were doing. I still don't know to this day if they if they got out of there.

I looked over the men on our flight. There were 237 men. I saw Infantry, Armor and Artillery men, Special Forces, Airborne, and Green Beret. There was so many that had it worse than I did. Some had endured much more. Would we be able to handle the world? There were many that knew they could not, so they extended for another tour in Vietnam. Some would just go crazy, unable ever to cope with all of it. One hundred thousand men and women have committed suicide since the war was over. There are over 1,000 Vietnam Veterans a year who are still committing suicide. Over 100,000 are homeless. Many believe if they had died in Vietnam, they would have at least died honorably. They have never been able to escape the nightmares and horrors they experienced in the war. I know that my strength came from my family. I didn't want to show that I wasn't tough enough to handle the world, no matter how difficult it was for me.

CHAPTER 14
GOING HOME; BEING "NORMAL"

So do not fear, I am with you; do not be dismayed, for I am your God. I will strengthen you and help you; I will uphold you with my righteous right hand.

All who rage against you will surely be ashamed and disgraced; those who oppose you will be as nothing and perish.

Though you search for your enemies, you will not find them. Those who wage war against you will be as nothing at all.

For I am the Lord, your God, who takes hold of your right hand and says to you, Do not fear; I will help you.
Isaiah 41:10–13

We landed in Oakland, California. There was a loud cheer from all the troops. We taxied around for a while. When the door opened, an E-8 Sgt. entered the plane telling us there was a 10-foot chain-link fence around the exit. He told us to stay on the yellow lines. "There are demonstrators outside. It is too far for you to be spit on, but they have water pistols full of bleach that will ruin your uniforms."

Welcome home, Soldier! I had gotten new dress greens with my name and rank and my Blackhorse patch on it. It was the first time I had worn my rank. Already an E-5 and I had never worn my rank. Anyway, I sure didn't want bleach on my dress uniform.

We got off the plane. It was December 19, 1968, and the weather seemed like it was freezing. A year with temperatures over 100 degrees every day made temperatures in the 40s seem like the deep freeze.

The demonstrators were yelling and trying to get to us. They were calling us everything from baby killers to orphan makers to warmongers, you name it. We were led into a large Plexiglas tunnel under the terminal to get our duffel bags. The buses would pick us up down there.

"Do not go in the regular terminal!" they cautioned us. It was two o'clock in the morning. How could things be so bad that we had to be protected? I couldn't believe it.

We were at an Air Force Base again for the rest of the night. The next morning, we cleared our paperwork and were taken back to the airport to try and catch a plane to Oklahoma City. They told us to spread out and not to tell people we had just come home from Vietnam. We had to fly on a commercial airline, but on military standby. Mike and I were both trying to get to Oklahoma City. We got bumped two flights in a row. There was one more flight that stopped everywhere in the world it seemed before landing in the city. We had both called home to tell our folks to meet us. My folks had to drive about three hours.

What a thrill to see them again! I was really wishing I hadn't handled my relationship with my fiancée so badly, because she wasn't there. I hugged them all. My complexion was so dark, and my hair had bleached out blond from the sun.

One of the first things my dad said to me was how much he appreciated me for not writing the things I had gone through. Mike had written a lot about it to his parents, and they had both nearly had a nervous breakdown. I just said he shouldn't have put them through that and didn't say any more.

I was so glad to be home. We went straight to my granny's house and two of my aunts and uncles were there, along with some of my cousins. My uncle had a big sign on his car that read, "Welcome home!" My dad told me that my family might be the only ones who welcomed me home. He said after World War II and the Korean Conflict that they had parades and respect from the whole country. "If you guys ever get thanked or appreciated, it will be a long time from now," he told me. I just felt comfortable for the first time in a long time. No one asked me much about Vietnam. I could tell my cousins had been told not to ask.

I remember wanting to smoke a cigarette so bad. Some of my relatives told me I should quit now that I was home. I'd never smoked around any of them so I was being respectful, but was not intending to quit.

We visited for two or three hours, and my folks had to work the next day, so we needed to travel the three hours back to their home in Southeastern Oklahoma. It was cold and getting dark. I thought we had better go. I probably sounded rude because my uncle said, "You can travel down the interstate at night using your headlights and go 65 or 70 mph." I had forgotten what that was like.

My granny asked me where I was going next, and I told her Ft. Sill after a 30-day leave. She told me that she had some things she needed done and had saved them for me. She said, "I knew when you left that you would be back. Prayer is a powerful tool, and I used it."

"Thank you, Gran!"

We left after dark for the trip to Southeastern Oklahoma. It felt so good to ride in a car. I slept some of the way home. I asked how my aunt and uncle were doing out in Arizona since they had lost their son. They told me how different their lives were now. I never told anyone how guilty I felt and still feel. I saw my uncle a year or so later and couldn't say anything. It was 25 years before I saw my Aunt, and still, I could say nothing.

We had a good Christmas and New Year. I was 21 years old now and trying to figure out how I could get back with my fiancée. My sister was getting married. She waited for me, and I made it. I was drinking and smoking and enjoying being home. I didn't watch any news or read the papers. I just wanted all that out of my head. My days went by too fast, and before I knew it, it was time for me to report to Fort Sill, Oklahoma.

My thoughts were still with the guys I left in Vietnam, wondering what happened to them. Ft. Sill sounded so good. I knew something about the fort being there from my Survey Training, plus it was also close to home. I was trying to rescue my relationship with my fiancée. She was still there for me. I know her dad had tried to tell her how much war affects one's judgment when one loses hope. God was working on my behalf in every part of my life, but as usual, I didn't know it.

CHAPTER 15
PLAYING "ARMY"

Blessed is the man who perseveres, under trial, because when he has stood the test, he will receive the crown of life that God has promised to those who love him. James 1:12

I had driven my car to the parking lot and reported to the 1st Srgt. I was still an E-5, but no longer a Sergeant. I was reporting to a missile unit and going to work in Survey as a Specialist E-5. That is what I had received my training for, 14 months previously.

I was in charge and had signed for thousands of dollars worth of equipment. I wore starched fatigues, shined boots, all my patches, rank and name sewn on . . . I was a real troop. The 1st Sergeant lined me out on all my duties and showed me a spotless motor pool where the survey vehicles were. The 1st Sgt. said the Captain wanted to see me.

"What for?"

"I don't know. His office is across the hall. He usually doesn't talk to anyone, so go find out."

I reported in and saluted him. "I'm reporting, as requested, Sir." He stuck out his hand for me to shake. That was real unusual in the states for an Officer to do. I noticed the Vietnam ribbon he wore, meaning he had served there.

"Sit down and relax." He asked about my tour in Vietnam. I told him about being in an Armor Unit and not being assigned to a Survey Unit. He was familiar with most of what I shared with him. He told me a little about what he had done, and we had been to some of the same places.

He said, "Son, this playing 'Army' after being in Vietnam is not easy, so if things start bothering you just come in and talk. My door is always open."

"Thank you, Sir. I'm trying real hard to keep it together."

I had been assigned a room, 10' x 10,' with four beds, a footlocker, and a small closet. There were two E-4s also in the room. They were complaining about the small room and living conditions. I said, "This is fine with me."

"The showers and stools are all the way at the other end of the hall!"

"Do the stools flush and is there hot water?"

They looked at each other. "Yes."

"That's great with me."

They were both drafted, one from California, the other from the state of Washington. They had been at Ft. Sill their entire time in service. They both had five months left. They were drafted about the same time I was. They would never go to Vietnam, but they griped all the time and had to walk to the end of the hall for a shower. It wasn't their choice that they hadn't gone to Vietnam. It was just the way things happened. I certainly didn't feel any anger or resentment toward them. They asked me about my Vietnam tour. I didn't tell them much. I didn't want to think about it, but I told them some of the things I had written home. I seemed to be okay, just shutting Vietnam out. I was still avoiding watching any news about it. I knew that Mike from FDC was assigned to a unit down the street from where I was. He had gotten married, and I hadn't seen him at all.

Jake, the guy that was in Vietnam when I was but assigned to Bien Hoa Air Base, was in the Unit next door. He had bought a new car. I saw him quite a bit. He was really a good guy. I was rolling along pretty well when the 1st Sgt. called me in to tell me they were putting together a funeral detail for the burial of GI's in the state of Oklahoma.

"You'll be on the firing squad."

I really wanted to start telling him all the reasons I didn't want to do that, but I just said, "Okay." In a couple of days, we gathered up to start practicing for the detail. I knew my being left-handed would prevent them from using me. The 1st Lt. in charge noticed me. He replaced me with a pallbearer, telling me I was the ranking pallbearer now. I practiced as the head pall-bearer and presented the flag. My plan hadn't worked, and this was even worse.

"Sir, I can't do that, especially Vietnam Veterans."

"You act like you were in a war instead of at a Base Camp somewhere. In this Army *can't* doesn't get it done. You start practicing with the pallbearers."

We practiced every day for two weeks before we began traveling all over Oklahoma for military funerals. The WWII, Korean, and other veterans that had died, but were never in a war or conflict I could handle, but the Vietnam Army Veterans with only a picture and a flag on the casket were so hard to bear. Almost all were married with young children. Some of the caskets were extremely heavy, and I knew there were probably just some body parts with some weights added. I was the only Vietnam Veteran in the group. Sometimes, some of them would say something or be disrespectful causing me to get really mad. I know they hadn't seen what I had and didn't have any way of knowing what I knew, but I thought our own troops should be more respectful of a Vietnam Veteran who had given his life for our Country. I also knew they were all just kids and didn't think or mean to sound the way they did.

I felt so guilty handing the folded flag to the mother or widow of a Veteran, and sometimes, I felt they hated me because they knew by my uniform I had been to Vietnam, and I had made it while their son or husband did not. I still wanted so much to reach out to them and let them know my heart was with them. This continued to be my duty for the next three months.

The Captain called me in and told me of an I.G. Inspection that our Unit was having in about two months. "I want everyone and everything to be ready. This is very important to me personally."

"Sir, I can plot targets, give coordinates, and I've been reading some books, but I can't run a Survey Crew. It's been 17 months since I was trained, and I haven't done it since."

"I figured that. That's why I called you in early. I will send you through a refresher course."

"Sir, we may not have time to do that and train a crew. There is a guy in the unit next door, and all he did was Survey. He knows what he is doing. If we could borrow him and give me three men, we can get this done."

"Okay, I know the Captain over there. I'll get him."

"Is he a Vietnam Vet?"

"Yes, but he surveyed on Bien Hoa Air Base."

"Jake will be here. You get this done, and I'll make you and Jake both Staff Sgt. E-6s. I have to pass this inspection. I have applied for flight school and without an excellent result, I won't be accepted."

"Sir, I know the way things work. I don't have enough time in service or time in grade of E-5 to make E-6, and as soon as my time is up, I'm getting out. But whatever happens, I will not let you down. I'll do the job. Sir, there is one thing. This funeral detail is bothering me. I'd like to get off of it."

"I'll tell the Lieutenant you're off it, and he can replace you. Son, I told you to come to me if you had any problems. You would never have been on that detail if I had known."

"Yes, Sir, but I didn't want to be complaining about everything."

"You're off it now."

"Thank you, Sir."

Jake began reporting to our Unit every morning and

working with me and three other guys. It went extremely well. The inspection would cover any of five different locations, so we plotted and surveyed all five in advance. With Jake's help, it went easily. When the day came for the big inspection, everything clicked perfectly. I had one old E-6 Sergeant who reminded me of Hines. He kept coming around looking at what I was doing. He was convinced I was plotting my targets wrong. I said, "Sgt., I did this for a year in Vietnam in combat. We weren't just playing Army. I know what I am doing. Don't be changing my targets!"

The Captain came over to see how I was doing. I told him about the Sgt. "I know," he told me. "He came and told me you were wrong."

"Sir, I am not wrong. If he changes my targets, we will bust the survey, okay?"

"Did anyone else look over your targets?"

"No, Sir. I know what I am doing."

"I hope so because my military future depends on this."

"I called in live artillery all the time, and I never killed any of our guys. Just relax, Sir!" I could tell he was nervous. He really wanted flight school. The next morning we had completed our field operation and inspection. The Captain called everyone together on the parade field reading off the results. Everyone had an excellent score. He was really happy and thanked us. He told me he was turning in my papers for promotion to E-6, and Jake's Captain was doing the same for him.

"I have my ticket to flight school." He asked me if I had ever considered Officer Candidate School.

"No, Sir. My Captain in Vietnam said he would get me in if I wanted to go. I just want out of the Army when my time is over. Good luck to you in flight school." I left never believing for a second I'd ever see E-6. I continued my duties as before, except for the funeral detail.

I had married my fiancée and things were going well. We

bought a mobile home and had it moved to a trailer park right outside of Ft. Sill. I was handling things pretty well.

I was walking down the hall one morning and the Captain was looking for me. He told me to report to the Colonel in Headquarters at 1400 hours.

"I'll be there."

"I'll be leaving next week for flight school. I got accepted."

"That's great, Sir."

"I hope you don't get through school, and they send you back to Vietnam."

"They could. My wife is worried about that already."

I walked into Headquarters at 1400 hours. There were several men sitting around, including Jake. I said, "What is this?"

Jake answered, "It looks like E-6 time."

"Oh, bull!" There were guys that looked like grandpas waiting to make E-6, 14 or 15 years in the Army. We were both just under two years, but it happened. The Captain had done what he said. I went back to my Unit, and the Captain was standing in the door smiling.

"I told you I'd get it done!"

"Yes, Sir, you did. I just couldn't see how."

"I turned in a waiver for time in service and time in grade. Your new wife needs to sew the Sergeant stripes on for you."

"She will. It feels great being Staff Sgt. E-6 stateside! In Vietnam, Gus and I did an E-6 job because Hines would not do it."

The older Sergeants were really jealous. They couldn't believe two twenty-year olds could be E-6, but we were, and we didn't let them bother us. "It's not our fault it took you so long!" That stuff went on all the time. As long as they didn't say things in front of the men, we just ignored it.

CHAPTER 16

HEADING FOR GERMANY!

. . . And we rejoice in the hope of the glory of God. Not only so, but we also rejoice in our sufferings, because we know that suffering produces perseverance; perseverance, character; and character, hope. Romans 5:2–4

Several months went by. My wife was pregnant. Everything seemed to be going fine. Then my orders came for Germany . . . another missile unit and only six months left in the Army. I could not believe it! Jake got orders and so did Mike. Jake and I were assigned to the same unit and Mike to a different one. I was hoping that since my wife was pregnant with our first child and I had been promoted to E-6 and the orders were for E-5, I might not have to go. Nothing I tried got me out of Germany. My wife had to move back in with her parents. We moved our trailer back to Oklahoma City. My E-6 pay was around $400.00 per month. The expense was pretty hard on us. At least the government was going to pay for our baby and medical expenses. It made no sense to me to go to Germany with six months left and replace guys with only six months left. Everyone that knew me tried to help me. It must have been written in stone somewhere. I had to go. It was the Army plan for Jake, Mike, and me. We all went to Ft. Sill for training, then Vietnam, then back to Fort Sill. Now, we were all three going to Germany.

My first son was born just a short while after I arrived in

Germany. He would be five months old before I could see him . . . just one more "Army" deal. Jake and I shared a large room on the third floor. It had a large radiator heater under an 8-foot window. The ice on the inside of the window never melted. In fact, I never saw the ground. It was covered with snow and ice all the time I was there. I could hardly walk across the parade field. We weren't there very long until we went to the field to play war. It was thirty-seven degrees below zero. I caught double pneumonia. They sent me to a field hospital for three days. I got up every morning at zero five hundred hours or 5 A.M. to change my sheets and make my bed. After three days, I still wasn't doing all that great, but they sent me back to the field ensuring that I didn't miss anything.

We finally finished and went back to our barracks in Nuremburg, Germany, the place where the Nuremburg trials were held. The building was unique. It was five stories high and seven stories below. All but two floors under us were flooded. In the court room areas there were large slabs of marble on the floors and walls, some with large swastikas on them. The wood looked like a deep red mahogany. I thought about all the history in that building and wanted to learn more, but we didn't have time for that. There was another I.G. Inspection to get ready for. The whole place was nervous. It was their big deal. Promotions depended upon this inspection for the Career Army guys. The older Sergeants really wanted Jake and me to mess up. They would call us the coke and cookie Army. None of them had ever been to Vietnam. I just ignored them. I didn't see any point in letting them get to me. I knew where I had been and what I had done. They were worried they might have to go, and I knew I was *never* going back.

The old Sergeant who ran the Survey Crew for five years was promoted to E-7, so Jake and I were in charge of the crew. There was really no problem with both Jake and me there, and the crew was a good one. The old Sergeant kept trying to get us to do it his way. He did it the same way for years, and we could do it so much easier so we didn't pay any attention to him. Jake was pretty blunt in telling him we knew what we were doing. "We have done this for real, not play war."

The older Sergeants joined in with him saying, "Let the instant NCOs mess up. Maybe they'll get busted back to where they should be!" We couldn't make those idiots understand we did not care. We were going to do our jobs and then be out of the Army in two months, throwing away what had taken them years to achieve. We went about our business getting ready for the I.G. Inspection.

I had drawn Officer of the Day duty on a weekend, which meant just keeping an eye on everything as the troops came in late at night, usually drunk. Saturday afternoon I looked up from the 1st Sergeant's desk and saw a two-star general looking right at me. He said, "You the Officer of the Day?"

"Yes, Sir!" He noticed my Blackhorse patch. I had already recognized him. He also wore a Blackhorse patch, symbol of the only fully Armored Cavalry Regiment in Vietnam. I knew all about him. He was George Patton III. In Vietnam, he was a Full Bird Colonel—a year later, a two-star General. He asked when I served there.

"I served under you and Major Marino."

"Did you know Captain Dales?"

"Yes, Sir, I was beside him when he was killed. He was a good man."

"Sgt., I'm not going to inspect this place like I came here to do and roll some heads."

"Thank you, Sir, and congratulations on making Major General."

"People who do their jobs usually get rewarded. If not, you wouldn't be E-6."

"Yes, Sir."

He left the office. I could hear troops yelling, "Attention!" all over the place. I had never spoken to a General before. I was nervous, but I knew there was no comparison between an E-6 and a General. In about thirty minutes, the phone started ringing off the wall. The Captain, First Sergeant, and a couple of Senior NCOs were scared to death. The First Sergeant asked if he inspected the barracks.

"Yes, he did."

" . . . and the motor pool?"

"He will let you know what he found. There were a couple of Captains writing stuff down." I had been treated so badly by some of those Sergeants I couldn't help but mess with them some. The First Sergeant came to his office about an hour later drilling me again about where the General went and what he said. He had never given me a hard time, so I told him his area was fine.

"The only area he really went after was Motor Pool and Armory. He didn't look at my area or yours. I served under him in Vietnam. He was extremely respectful to me. He knew where I'd been. First Sergeant, you're okay, he just made a random check of those two areas."

I was having so much fun messing with the two Sergeants from those two areas. They were two of the Senior Sergeants that had given me a hard time. "The Armory and Motor Pool will get a written report later."

The Sergeants came to me and wanted to know everything. I said, "He'll have a written report to your Captain in a few days."

"Did you send him to our areas?"

"Oh, yeah, I'm going to tell a two-star General where to inspect!"

"Well, did he inspect the Survey area?"

"No, he didn't mess with me. I served under him in Vietnam. He wears the same patch I do. I was in the same firefights he directed. He's a pretty good guy." They were turning green.

We continued to work on our exercise. It seemed like everything was in good shape and ready to go. We went back to the field and set up. The I. G. Inspectors showed up. We got our locations, and Jake came over to me and said, "Let's do a good job."

"We'll do all right."

"That's Sgt. Brown. We were in the same unit in Vietnam. He'll be fair with us. We shouldn't have any problems, anyway." I did tell him about the old Sergeant wanting us to do it his way. We completed the survey and plotted all the targets. It really went smoothly. When you're relaxed and know you're leaving anyway, things just go well.

One of the old Sergeants couldn't wait to tell me in the Mess Hall in front of everyone that the survey crew probably messed up and would bring everyone's score down. "How did we do that, Sgt.?"

"Your instrument operator took his steel pot off every time he looked through the transit for a reading." The old Survey Chief had to tell me he never let his men take their steel pots off while viewing or at any time. I just sat there for a while and started to let it go, but I was so sick of those guys.

"You know, in Vietnam you could take your steel pot off or turn your hat backwards to make sure you got an accurate reading. Is the manual different over here where we are just playing war? I just figured it was the same Army manual. You never know, though. I mean Patton was a Full Colonel a year ago, and now he's a Two-star General inspecting Motor Pools and Armories."

The next week we were called into the theater for the results of the I.G. Inspections. The old Sergeants were so sure we had messed up that they were looking around to make sure Jake and I were there. We could hardly wait. We felt sure we would get a good report, and if not, we had only six weeks left in the Army. The Lt. Colonel read the overall rating. The average was Excellent. The individual ratings were:

Communication—Excellent
Survey—Excellent

Motor Pool—Good

Armory—Good

Everyone else received marks of Excellent. How ironic! Those two Sergeants had the lowest scores. They didn't turn around and look at us. Then they read two areas of Special Commendation; they had Supply and Survey to stand. He read the survey was unique and used a new method of triangulation to pinpoint accuracy over snow-covered mountains. All targets were hit within one meter. I thought those guys were going to throw up. Jake and I knew we did a good job and that Jake's buddy had just thrown all that other stuff in. The Motor Pool Sergeant was so mad you could see him boiling. I said, "Hey, Sergeant, I thought you did a good job on the motor pool. The survey vehicles looked great." If he ever spoke to me after that, I don't remember it.

CHAPTER 17
HIDING MY FEELINGS

Do not merely listen to the word, and so deceive your-selves. Do what it says. Anyone who listens to the word but does not do what it says is like a man who looks at his face in a mirror and, after looking at himself, goes away and immediately forgets what he looks like. James 1:22–24

My Army days were almost over. It had been a long three years. I had a five-month-old son I had never seen. My wife was struggling financially. I wanted a normal life, if I could have it. I wanted to be a family man. It turned out to be a lot harder than I thought it would be. I flew to Ft. Dix, New Jersey, and processed out. Jake and I were the only E-6s getting out. There were probably 300 GIs in the room.

I started going to school at night and working at a grocery store in the daytime, plus getting adjusted to being a father. I got a job back in construction—carpentry and home building. I really enjoyed it. I was still trying to wash my Vietnam experience away with beer and cigarettes. It bothered my wife and son. They both had asthma, but I did it anyway.

I had been hearing of the good government jobs for Vietnam Vets. I went to Tinker Air Force Base to apply for a job with benefits. I was treated like anyone off the street. The guy interviewing was not a Vietnam Veteran. He reminded me of another Sgt. Hines. He was upset that he had to try and place

Veterans in a job. I felt he made no effort to help me and just said, "I have your application. If anything comes up, I'll call you." I felt really out of place. I had lost three years of my life . . . enough time to have finished college. I had a wife and baby to support, and I was being treated with no respect, something I had at least earned in the Military. There was just something about being on a Military Base and being treated like that that really upset me. I knew I wasn't wearing my E-6 stripes any more, but it was hard to accept the treatment and trying to start over. I was determined to do what I needed to do and not have a chip on my shoulder because of my experience in Vietnam. I walked out of his office thanking him.

As I was walking out through a large waiting room of hopeful applicants, I spotted a guy I went to high school with. It was a total shock, because I had been told he was killed in Vietnam. I had to notice the burn scars on his face and arm. He showed me his chest, burned with white phosphorous, the same kind of mortar that landed beside me but didn't go off. It brought back memories in one instant of all the burning bodies I had seen. I thought I could smell that awful smell of burning flesh. I knew then that one thing I could not do was any job involving rescue, like a police officer, fireman, or emergency worker. He could tell it bothered me and told me he was sorry. I told him, "I have to get used to the world. I can't let everything get to me."

I never wanted to see a car wreck and hoped I would never be needed to help someone. I felt if I could just stay away from that stuff I could shut it out. There has been no way to shut out the war—the burning of children in Waco, the Oklahoma City bombing, and the Twin Towers. I know by listening to the interviews of the rescue workers that they also carry deep scars from such traumatic events.

The government job never did happen. I worked construction, joined the Carpenter's Union, and started teaching Apprentice Training Classes. A couple of years later, I was able to go into business for myself. My second son had been born. I was still drinking and smoking. My wife had shown such great tolerance and understanding with me.

I really liked being self-employed and started building custom homes. I was making my family a good living and was very proud of that. I felt like I was handling the world. I had two sons to raise, and I had to stop drinking and do a better job of being a good dad. I began coaching the little league teams, and going to everything my sons were involved in. My job was perfect for me. I could schedule my time around the practices and games and always be there for them. (The Specialists have since told me that was exactly what I needed to do, stay busy and become involved with other things.) I had a great amount of freedom being self-employed. I think a regular 8 to 5 job would have been very difficult for me. This way, I was able to stay away from most people. If I had a jerk to work for, it didn't last long, and I could go back to my place of peace. I was staying involved and was very proud of my family.

CHAPTER 18
SEARCHING FOR SOMETHING

"Come, all you who are thirsty, come to the waters;
Why spend money on what is not bread, and your labor
on what does not satisfy? . . . Listen, listen to me, and eat what is
good, and your soul will delight in the richest of fare. Give ear
and come to me; hear me, that your soul may live."
Isaiah 55: 1,2–3

I was sliding through life pretty well. I didn't tell anyone I was a Vietnam Veteran and didn't get involved in any conversations. Most of what I heard was from guys who were never there, just acting like they were. I still felt like I was walking on eggshells. I knew that any anger coming from me would not be good. I don't mean just getting a little mad or upset. I'm talking about having a built up hardness of my heart towards others. No one ever knew what I was hiding. I was seeing Vets getting divorced, doing drugs, drinking heavily, living on the streets, crying out for help, and just carrying Vietnam on their sleeves. I thought if I can hide this stuff, they should be able to also. I had the answers . . . or so I thought. I still didn't realize that I was just a walking time bomb.

Everyone's reality is different. Until you have jumped from a chopper with bullets flying over your head, you don't know what kind of an individual, what kind of a man you really are. Everyone's breaking point is not the same. It doesn't mean you have more or less courage than someone else. It just means that people face reality at different times in their lives, but eventually, all must face it if they want to get better. My greatest strength came from my family. They were trying to reach out to me and help me cope, but not really understanding what I was hiding. I am able to write because God is guiding me and giving me strength to reach out and help others—reaching for that understanding that maybe has not been there before. The Vietnam experience of a Veteran is so difficult, and sometimes so misunderstood because we have been unable to share it. We have hidden so much for so long. My own family is learning much of this for the first time.

When my boys were in junior high and high school, they were doing well. My oldest son was good enough in basketball to receive a college scholarship. My youngest son played football, was president of the Future Farmers of America, and was elected to Who's Who in Junior Colleges. They both were very popular, and their rooms were lined with trophies they had won. All my thoughts were on my family and watching my sons grow into young men.

I became very disgusted with Jimmy Carter when he gave full pardons to draft dodgers (even the ones that burned American flags and went to Canada). What a slap in the face to all of those men and women whose names are now on the Wall! I thought if Mr. Carter would visit a Veteran's home and talk to some of those paralyzed for life, those with missing limbs, or those left with severe emotional and mental problems caused by the war, he might think differently about pardoning the draft dodgers. Humanitarianism should be shown to our loyal Countrymen first and foremost. I was so thankful when a man of strength and courage took his place for eight years to rebuild our Military and accomplish so much. When the Gulf War happened, I was concerned for my sons and nephews. They were taught great respect for our Country and for Veterans. They all call me every Veteran's Day. It means so much to me. I thanked every Veteran I knew that was involved in Desert Storm. They were exposed to toxic gases. Some of the suits they had for protection were full of holes and defective (Made in China).

Then something happened in this Country that I thought would be impossible. A draft dodger was elected President, a person who was called Commander-in-Chief of the Military. I knew Veterans that voted for him. The ones I knew weren't Combat Veterans. They were Vietnam Era Veterans, meaning they were in the military while the war was going on, but never involved in the fighting. It bothered me that they would disgrace themselves in such a way. Some of the President's policies (which were totally against everything I believed in) were discussed while he was standing in front of the Vietnam Wall. I was trying so hard not to let hate consume me. It seemed this brought about so much pain and a hardening of my heart. I wanted to forgive, but it just seemed to get harder.

When my grandmother was 94 years old (born in 1900), she was such a godly person. My wife was caring for her several hours a day when she started needing constant care. She had days when she would forget who we were. One evening I walked into her small home. She was bright and alert. She said, "I need to talk to you right now." She feared she might slip back into forgetfulness. She continued, "God has a plan for your life. You need to seek Him and find out what your assignment is. Don't let what has happened to you leave you with a hardened heart. You are special. God has kept a covering over you all of your life. You need to have a daily walk with Jesus." She took my hand and started praying for me. I was never so touched. I felt my heart change, and I could feel the presence of Jesus. She passed away in 1995, the same year my dad died.

I had not led my family as I should have in spiritual things. I was pretty liberal with my sons because I understood how quickly freedom could be taken away. A young preacher had a church a few miles away from where we lived. He was a little different than we were accustomed to in our small town.

He rode a Harley and carried his Bible everywhere he went. He started reaching the young people in town. What a blessing he was!

It was just a short time until my oldest son, his wife, and my grandson were attending church there. My oldest son had become a youth minister, and my youngest son was the praise and worship leader and even went on a mission's trip to Peru and the Philippines. We were going regularly, I was doing the announcements, and my wife was volunteering to cook for the senior citizens every Tuesday at the church.

CHAPTER 19
PULLING THE TRIGGER

Streams of tears flow from my eyes because my people are destroyed. My eyes will flow unceasingly, without relief, until the Lord looks down from heaven and sees.

Those who were my enemies without cause hunted me like a bird. They tried to end my life in a pit and threw stones at me; the waters closed over my head, and I thought I was about to be cut off.

I called on your name, O Lord, from the depths of the pit. You heard my plea: "Do not close your ears to my cry for relief." You came near when I called you and you said, "Do not fear." O Lord, you took up my case; you redeemed my life. Lamentations 3: 48–50; 52–58

My problems with Vietnam were getting worse. Some of the men in the church were noticing it and trying to help me. I just couldn't share with them the way I am sharing now by writing.

During this time in my life, I was coming home from work when I saw a truck hit a car in front of me. There were three young boys in the car and I tried to get them out. The car was in flames, and I couldn't get to them. There was nothing I could do but stand there as they burned. That moment pulled the trigger on thirty years I had buried deep within. I read in the paper where one of the boy's last names was the same as my wife's maiden name. That really bothered me.

Soon after everything began falling apart. If I smelled anything unusual burning in the trash like plastic or dog hairs or if I heard any loud noises, I would jump and become very nervous. I began having flashbacks and nightmares that would leave me trembling and soaking wet from sweat. I sank into a deep depression.

My family, once again, was trying to help me. I don't mean just my immediate family but my wife's family as well. Everyone was concerned. There was so much love coming to me from everyone. My sister spent hours on the internet trying to find out some way to help me. My wife took me to the VA to see a psychiatrist. That was the first time in over thirty years that I had been to a VA facility. I just didn't want to do anything that might remind me of my years in the service, but we had become desperate. I had to have some help. We were about to lose everything we had worked for all of our lives. My boys were helping us. Everyone was.

They told me at the VA I had PTSD (Post Traumatic Stress Disorder) and agent orange poisoning. All my life it seemed I had been tough enough, but now it was my turn to break. I cried every day. I thought about Vietnam all the time. I couldn't do anything. I was rude and indifferent to the people I loved the most. I just wanted to be left alone. It seemed like no one really understood why I had lost control and why I was acting that way, especially after all these years. How could they have known? I never talked about it, and I had always been able to handle everything by myself.

I thought about Bear and Harlem. I still don't know if they got out alive or not. I knew Gus didn't make it, and now I was wondering if I did. I had three or four years of pure misery. I told my sons I didn't know why God had brought me home, but maybe it was to have two sons like them. They were serving God and were both fine, young Christian men. I have two wonderful grandchildren, handsome, young Zechariah True and my beautiful granddaughter, Cassidy. Maybe this was my purpose.

CHAPTER 20

SEEKING HELP AND UNDERSTANDING

Humble yourselves, therefore, under God's mighty hand that he may lift you up in due time. Cast all your anxiety on him because he cares for you. Be self-controlled and alert. Your enemy the devil prowls around like a roaring lion looking for someone to devour. Resist him, standing firm in the faith, because you know that your brothers throughout the world are undergoing the same kind of sufferings.

And the God of all grace, who called you to his eternal glory in Christ, after you have suffered a little while, will himself restore you and make you strong, firm and steadfast. To him be the power for ever and ever. Amen. 1 Peter 5:6–10

The end of all things is near. Therefore be clear minded and self-controlled so that you can pray. Above all, love each other deeply, because love covers over a multitude of sins. Offer hospitality to one another without grumbling. Each one should use whatever gift he has received to serve others, faithfully administering God's grace in its various forms. 1 Peter 4:7–10

I'm 55 years old now, and I've shed so many tears remembering and trying to write this. God has led me to do this. I've seen so many Vietnam Vets in trouble trying to make it. I'm writing this mostly for the families . . . to help you understand

185

what happened to us over there. None of us want pity. We just need understanding.

When I've given my testimony, people start crying almost as soon as I start talking. They will tell me later about their brothers, sons, or husbands, and they want to know what they can do to help them. I know it's difficult to understand how our hearts could become so hard and calloused, but we would have never been able to do what we did, otherwise. I could never have done the things I was asked to do if I had been filled with the Holy Spirit. God is still working his plan through me. His angels were protecting and teaching me. The strength to write this comes from my Jesus, and I am receiving healing right now. If I wasn't, I wouldn't continue because it is so difficult to remember all the pain and suffering I felt and witnessed in Vietnam.

After saying that my purpose was to have wonderful sons and grandchildren, a lady stood up and told me God had a lot more for me. She said, "God has a special mission and plan for your life." I was trying to figure it out on my own, going to doctors, getting pills, and being told I'd never be any better . . . I'd never improve. When I finally let God do everything and I got myself out of the way, every part of my life began changing. Every door was opening, and I knew what I was supposed to do. I started meeting with a group of Combat Vietnam Veterans weekly, all of them Army or Marine Vets. What a brotherhood of men we have . . . such closeness. We all have our Harlems, Bears, and Guses, but most of all we have an understanding of each other, and we can relate to one another's feelings.

I have been able to witness to them. Some have started going to church where I attend. Some of them had it much worse than I did. Some maybe not as bad, but we all have the scars and wounds of combat and share feelings of guilt and shame we are now trying to overcome.

Our motorcycle preacher has moved to Texas, and I heard he has a service once a week for Vietnam Veterans. God has made it possible for me to help Veterans. There are so many out there who need to be reached. God moved in my life. He sent angels to protect me, and I have kept them very busy. I have a daily walk with Jesus, and I know He is always with me.

I have learned that guilt and war go together. I tried to live in quietness and shut it out. *Sometimes I can still see the enemies' eyes before killing them. I no longer feel the coldness and hardness in my heart I once felt. The wounds of war seem to always bleed. Finally, I learned to let Jesus put his healing hand over mine.*

Epilogue

Never Ending War
It's been 31 years; why did it come back?
I stand here and look at the wall so black.
Some of my friends' names in granite,
I just know I'll never understand it!
We'd lie in the jungle sprayed with agent orange,
Not knowing it would hurt us or our newborn.
We didn't think our government would lie.
We just knew we had to fight - or die.
We may have killed children, no fault of our own,
But we live with this daily and suffer alone.
We didn't know there would be a Wall;
If our names were on it, didn't matter at all.
We were just doing what we thought was right,
But we could not see any end in sight.
As I sit at this table with brothers of mine,
We need to be healed, but it takes so much time.
Because we went to fight and serve,
We now must fight for the rights we deserve.
I thank God for this group of Vietnam Vets,
Not one of them has let me down yet.
I find peace with Jesus and a group of good men.
I pray daily for each one of them.
S/Sgt. Bill Draper
U. S. Army, 11th Armored Cavalry
Vietnam
December 1967 - December 1968

END NOTES

[1]   Department of Veterans Affairs' Website

Contact William C. Draper
or order more copies of this book at

TATE PUBLISHING, LLC

127 East Trade Center Terrace
Mustang, Oklahoma 73064

(888) 361 - 9473

Tate Publishing, LLC

www.tatepublishing.com